Discovering
KINGS AND QUEENS

D. E. Wickham

Shire Publications Ltd

CONTENTS

The earliest monarchs	...	...	...	...	...	3
The Normans ...	...	...	...	...	...	5
The Plantagenets	...	...	...	...	...	9
Lancaster and York	...	...	...	...	...	20
The Tudors ...	...	...	...	...	...	28
The Stuarts ...	...	...	...	...	...	57
The Hanoverians	...	...	...	...	...	71
The twentieth century	...	...	...	...	...	80
Some royal foreigners	...	...	...	...	...	83
Index	...	...	...	...	...	84

ACKNOWLEDGEMENTS

Photographs are credited as follows: Fiona and Keith Baverstock, plate 17; Robert Bristow, plate 10; Robert Glover, plate 23; George H. Haines, plates 2, 14, 16, 18; Cadbury Lamb, plates 3, 4, 6, 12, 19, 22, 24; Raymond Lea, plates 7, 25; John A. Long, plate 21; Jane Miller, plate 11; Mrs. E. Preston, plate 20; Brian Shuel, plates 8, 9; F. Spalding-Smith, plate 15; David Uttley, plate 13; J. W. Whitelaw, plate 5; Geoffrey N. Wright, plate 1.

The cover illustration is a detail from the painting 'The Happier Days of Charles I' by Frederick Goodall (1848-1871), reproduced by kind permission of the Libraries and Arts Department of the Metropolitan Borough of Bury. The painting is on view at Bury Art Gallery and Museum.

Printed in Great Britain by C. I. Thomas & Sons (Haverfordwest) Ltd, Press Buildings, Merlins Bridge, Haverfordwest.

This book is not intended as a brief history of the reigns of British monarchs but as a guide to the many places in Britain that are associated with them. Most of the places described are open to the public. When in doubt, use the annual *Historic Houses, Castles and Gardens,* of which a new edition is available each January.

THE EARLIEST MONARCHS

Boadicea, or Boudicca, revolted against the Romans in A.D. 61. Her tribe, the Iceni, from Norfolk, massacred the inhabitants of Roman **Colchester,** sacked **St. Albans** and **London,** and almost annihilated the Ninth Legion. Her modern memorial, showing her famous scythe-wheeled chariot, is on the best site in Britain, at the end of **Westminster Bridge,** and her grave, according to legend, is under Platform 10 of **King's Cross** railway station.

Between A.D. 10 and 40, **Colchester** had been the capital of the dominant British chieftain Cunobelin, Shakespeare's Cymbeline, father of the celebrated Caractacus. Two centuries later Colchester was the birthplace of Helena, the daughter of King Coel, Old King Cole of the nursery rhyme. She became the mother of Constantine the Great, a major influence in persuading her son to make the Roman Empire Christian, and a saint who 'discovered' the True Cross.

Elizabeth II is a direct descendant of Sceaf, a semi-legendary chieftain in Schleswig and the Baltic lands, who lived twenty-four generations before Cerdic, an historical king of the West Saxons who died in A.D. 534. For the next five hundred years an amazing series of kings and chiefs ruled in Britain.

The legend of Arthur probably commemorates a Romanised British chief of about A.D. 600, but imagination brings him near to us in the West Country. His supposed cliff-top castle at **Tintagel** in Cornwall, fulfils all one's hopes, though his real stronghold may have been the fort revealed by excavations at **South Cadbury,** Somerset. His grave is said to be marked by a stone near Slaughter Bridge at **Camelford,** Cornwall, but he was reputedly reburied with Queen Guinevere in **Glastonbury Abbey** (plate 1) and the site is marked in the ruins there, the heart of Avalon.

The future Pope Gregory's meeting with English slave-boys—'not Angles but angels'—brought St. Augustine to Ebbsfleet, **Pegwell Bay,** in Kent in 597. He was received by Ethelbert, king of Kent, whose Frankish wife Bertha was already a Christian, worshipping in a chapel with Roman walls. This chapel is now the chancel of St. Martin's church, **Canterbury,** the oldest parish church in Britain. King, queen and saint are buried in St. Augustine's Abbey, Canterbury.

King Osric of Mercia lies in a pleasant sixteenth-century tomb in **Gloucester Cathedral** because he founded the first monastery there in 681. His effigy holds a model of the church. Over a century later his successor Offa of Mercia built **Offa's Dyke,** a marvellous earthwork running for 120 miles from **Prestatyn** to a point on the Wye opposite **Chepstow,** showing the boundary between his kingdom and the Welsh. It still roughly marks the border of England and Wales.

Egbert of Wessex became Bretwalda or overlord of the English in 827, largely as a result of defeating the Mercians at Ellendun, now known as **Wroughton,** south of Swindon in Wiltshire in 825. This Wessex supremacy continued under Ethelbald and Ethelbert, both buried behind the high altar in **Sherborne Abbey,** Dorset, and under their younger brother Alfred the Great. He was born in 849 at **Wantage,** Oxfordshire, where a statue in the market-place reminds us of another in his capital, **Winchester.** He defeated Guthrum's Danes at **Ethandun,** a battle fought in 878 on Salisbury Plain. In the Ashmolean Museum at **Oxford** is the magnificent Alfred Jewel, a treasure of gold and cloisonné enamel, possibly Alfred's personal possession. It was found near **Athelney** in Somerset, a district he frequently visited, and its inscription runs *Aelfred mec heht gewyrcan* — Alfred ordered me to be made.

Seven Saxon kings were crowned at **Kingston upon Thames,** on the coronation stone now given a granite base and iron railings, which stands outside the new Guildhall. Nevertheless, petty kings still reigned, the most famous being Edmund of East Anglia, martyred in 870 by Danish raiders who made him a target for their arrows. He was interred at **Bury St. Edmunds** in Suffolk where the later abbey church is in ruins.

4

It is said that his bones now rest in the Duke of Norfolk's chapel at **Arundel Castle.**

Athelstan is said to lie in a fifteenth-century tomb in the abbey church at **Malmesbury,** Wiltshire. Eight British princes rowed Edgar the Peaceful along the river **Dee** as a mark of his supremacy in a reign free from war. He was crowned undisputed king of all England at **Bath** in May 973 and is buried at **Glastonbury.** Edward the Martyr, who was murdered in 979 by his stepmother on the fortified hilltop in Dorset now surmounted by the ruins of **Corfe Castle,** may be buried in the ruins of **Shaftesbury Abbey.**

The Danes conquered Britain. If Canute the Great really ordered the waves to go back as a rebuke to his courtiers' flattery, he probably did so at **Southampton,** or at **Bosham,** Sussex, where his daughter lies. Canute died at **Shaftesbury** and is buried in **Winchester Cathedral,** in one of the mortuary chests on the choir screen. The chests also contain his queen Emma, Edred, Egbert and possibly other kings of Wessex and all England—perhaps even Alfred.

The patron saint of early medieval England, Edward the Confessor, was born at **Islip** in Oxfordshire and is buried in **Westminster Abbey,** which he founded. His body remains in its shrine. His successor was Harold II, usually accepted as the last king before the Norman Conquest, since Edgar Atheling had no power. On 25th September 1066 Harold defeated the Norwegians under Hardrada at **Stamford Bridge,** across the river Derwent, in Humberside, a site marked by a memorial stone inscribed in English and Norwegian. Three days later Duke William of Normandy landed at **Pevensey** in Sussex and Harold made forced marches to meet him in battle at **Hastings** on 14th October. Harold was defeated. Originally buried at Hastings, his remains were translated to **Waltham Abbey** in Essex which he had founded.

THE NORMANS

William I (1066-1087)

Born in 1027 or 1028; bastard son of a tanner's daughter and Robert the Devil, Duke of Normandy; succeeded his father as Duke in 1035 aged about 7; king of England by right of conquest in 1066; died in 1087.

Exactly what Edward the Confessor promised his cousin Duke William of Normandy may never be clear, but William decided that he was entitled to the English throne and won it at the battle of **Hastings** on 14th October 1066, the best-known date and perhaps the most important single event in English history.

The story that Harold was killed by an arrow in the eye may be untrue, caused by misinterpretation of the Bayeux Tapestry, but he certainly fell dying near a spot where the altar of **Battle Abbey** afterwards stood, on Senlac Hill near Hastings. William vowed to build an abbey on the battlefield if he was victorious and this Benedictine minster became one of England's richest monastic houses. It was suppressed by Henry VIII, and only fragments of the original buildings remain above ground. The later fabric now houses a school but from its terrace one has a fine view of the battlefield, and Harold's monument is nearby.

Soon afterwards William accepted the submission of the country at **Berkhamsted Castle** and came to London for his coronation on Christmas Day 1066, the first to be held in the new **Westminster Abbey**. It was not until about 1078 that he began building the White Tower, still standing as the centre of Britain's most famous fortress, the **Tower of London**. We should not regard it merely as a sight for tourists: it has never been captured, it is strong enough to hold the Crown Jewels, and it was used as a state prison as recently as the Second World War.

As his security increased, William could turn to other matters. He loved the high deer as if he were their father, says a chronicler, and he cleared the **New Forest** to form a royal hunting area. Then he wanted to know the full extent of his acquisitions and, traditionally during his Christmas court of 1085 held in an earlier chapter house of **Gloucester Cathedral,** he ordered a survey to be made of his realm. This masterpiece of the Norman civil service was finished by 1086 and its two volumes are now in the **Public Record Office Museum** in Chancery Lane, London. They showed William the scope and nature of his new kingdom, its history, ownership and value, and how taxes could be fairly divided. All disputes of land tenure were decided by reference to it and there was no redress against it. By the early twelfth century it was called *Domesday Book* from the old English *dom*, meaning ' judgement '—so the belief that it was named because its statements were as final as Doomsday is more or less correct.

William the Conqueror married Matilda of Flanders, a

descendant of Alfred the Great, but he was not an English king. Like many of his immediate successors he was born in Normandy, at Falaise, died there and was buried there, at Caen.

William II (1087-1100)

Born in 1056; king in 1087 as third son and joint heir of William I; died in 1100.

Born in Normandy, William II, called Rufus for his ginger hair and scarlet face, is reputed to have had a vicious temper and a cruel and oppressive mind. His **Westminster Hall,** one of the few remnants of the medieval palace of Westminster, is a splendid building, nearly 240 feet long by 68 feet wide. He built it in 1097-9, boasting that it was a mere bedchamber to the palace which was to rise beside it. The walls have been refaced, however, and the best part of the hall, its glorious hammerbeam roof, was erected three hundred years later by Richard II (see page 19).

William's elder brother Richard had been killed by a stag in the New Forest in 1081, but both brothers loved hunting and were likely to hunt in the favourite royal forest. It would therefore not seem sinister that the king met his death while hunting in the **New Forest** on 2nd August 1100, but the deeper one seeks, the more suspicious one becomes. William died from an arrow in the chest. Was it fired accidentally, ricocheting from an oak-tree as suggested by the monument erected on the probable spot by Lord de la Warr in 1745 (plate 2)? Was the king a ritual sacrifice to the old religion of witchcraft? Was the arrow fired by an unknown hand? Was it fired by Walter Tirel, who was nearby and immediately fled the country—and conveniently became an ancestor of the man said to have murdered the princes in the Tower (see page 25)?

Whatever the details, the king's death was seen as the direct intervention of Heaven. Partly for that reason, and partly for the more general hatred they bore him, the local clergy bundled him into a grave before the high altar in **Winchester Cathedral** without ceremony or religious rites. A plain black coped tombstone was placed over the grave and no other memorial or royal effigy was ever set upon it. The cathedral tower collapsed seven years later and that too was seen as heavenly intervention, this time a protest against the burial. It was rebuilt.

Henry I (1100-1135)

Born in 1068 or 1070; succeeded his elder brother William II in 1100; died in 1135.

It is not clear whether Henry I was surnamed 'Beauclerc' because he was truly learned or because, in an age when such talents were rare among the upper classes, he could write his own name. The fourth son of William I, he was born at Selby in Yorkshire and gained popularity among the native English by marrying Matilda of Scotland, a granddaughter of the Anglo-Saxon king Edmund Ironside. Apart from that his reign is largely darkness lit with flashes of purple. He had at least twenty illegitimate children by six mistresses. He collected a menagerie at Woodstock. He died in Normandy of a fever which developed from acute indigestion after a surfeit of lampreys, a fish he ate whenever possible but which invariably disagreed with him.

His body was brought home to lie in **Reading Abbey,** the Benedictine house that he had founded in 1121 but which was not completed until 1164 when it was consecrated by Thomas Becket (plate 3). Reading Abbey became one of the richest and most powerful English abbeys, surpassed only by Glastonbury and St. Albans. Its church may have been larger than Westminster Abbey but it was suppressed by Henry VIII and became a quarry. The stone facing was removed from its walls so that only their flint filling remains, but the Inner Gateway has been heavily restored and houses paintings of events in the abbey's history. Henry's grave was destroyed at the Suppression but its place before the high altar is marked by a cross.

Stephen (1135-1154)

Born between 1097 and 1104; king in 1135 as Henry I's sister's son; died in 1154.

The reign of Stephen, who was born at Blois in France, was dominated by a series of rebellions, mostly about the Empress Matilda, forming a period so terrible that men believed Christ and his saints slept.

In the choir at **Hereford Cathedral** stands the chair reputedly if improbably used by Stephen at his royal proclamation there on Whit Sunday 1138. Our only other memory of him is his tomb. He and his queen, another Matilda, were buried in the abbey he founded at **Faversham** in Kent. The royal graves were destroyed when the abbey was suppressed, and their contents thrown into the nearby creek. A plaque in the church of

St. Mary of Charity, Faversham, records an unlikely tradition that the bones were afterwards placed there. All that remains of the abbey is part of the outer gateway, made into a house that later belonged to the mayor Thomas Arden, whose murder was dramatised in the Elizabethan tragedy *Arden of Feversham.*

Matilda
Born in 1102; daughter of Henry I; died in 1167.

The Empress Matilda is the least known of our monarchs though she definitely reigned as *Domina* or Lady of the English for six months during 1141.

Born in London, she was married to the German emperor Henry V from 1114 until his death in 1125. After her brother William was drowned in the White Ship in 1120, their father Henry I persuaded the nobles, led by his nephew Stephen, to swear allegiance to Matilda. At this period in English history, however, the heir to the throne was still the man able to claim it most effectively and Henry's death in 1135 merely began a civil war between Stephen and Matilda.

The best known incident of the war occurred during 1142 when Stephen besieged Matilda in **Oxford Castle.** One winter night after three months' stalemate, she put on white robes and escaped across the frozen river Isis, riding through the snow to **Wallingford,** Oxfordshire. The starving garrison surrendered and the castle had made its sole contribution to national history. Oxford Castle was built in the 1070s but was ruinous by the early thirteenth century. Only St. George's Tower still stands. It was perhaps the chapel bell-tower, but today, ironically, it stands in a back street by the county jail. Matilda died in France and is buried in Rouen Cathedral.

THE PLANTAGENETS

Henry II (1154-1189)
Born in 1133; son of the Empress Matilda and her second husband Geoffrey Plantagenet, Count of Anjou; by the Treaty of Wallingford agreed between Stephen and Matilda in 1153, Henry was declared heir to the throne; succeeded on Stephen's death in 1154; died in 1189.

When considering Henry II one realises how foreign the royalty and nobility of this country were, even in the late twelfth century. Henry was king of England, yet his background was French and, as there were royal estates in France, he was born at Le Mans, died at Chinon, and was buried at Fontevrault. England was very much part of a cosmopolitan kingdom, almost sharing a foreign king.

The king's mistress was Fair Rosamund Clifford, *Rosa Munda sed non Rosa Mundi*—not the Rose of the World. A well called after her (plate 4) and the traditional site of her bower are in the centre of the park at **Blenheim Palace**, though the last remains of her old palace at **Woodstock** were destroyed when Blenheim was built. She had been educated at **Godstow** nunnery beside the Thames a mile or two north of Oxford, once consecrated in the presence of King Stephen. She lived at the nunnery for a while, died there and was buried there in about 1176. Her monument in the choir was the richest of all those in the church—the shocked authorities had it removed as early as 1197. Godstow nunnery became a private house at the Dissolution of the monasteries and was burned down in 1646. Today only the boundary wall and the shell of a chapel survive.

Henry is historically overshadowed by Saint Thomas Becket. Of relatively humble birth, Becket obtained the king's personal friendship and rose to high political office. Created Archbishop of Canterbury specifically to act as the royal tool, Becket at once defended the Church against the Crown, depriving Henry of support which previous occurrences suggested that he had every right to expect.

Angevin tempers were always short and, in 1170, a few chance and hasty words from Henry encouraged four knights to return to England and slay the 'turbulent priest' in the north-west transept of his own **Canterbury Cathedral**. Europe's collective conscience was stunned. The stricken Henry realised that now the Church was bound to win and he conceded all its demands. Dying for his religious beliefs, at least in a loose sense, the worldly Becket was accounted a saint and miracle worker even before his canonisation in 1173. The following summer Henry walked as a barefoot penitent to be scourged by the Canterbury monks before his old adversary's tomb. The cathedral choir was rebuilt to give maximum effect to a new shrine especially created for the martyr's remains which were translated from a grave in the cathedral crypt in 1220. The shrine became the chief object of popular pilgrimage in Britain for three hundred years, in all Europe perhaps second only to Rome, but was stripped of its decoration by Henry VIII and the tomb destroyed. Nowadays one can see the Pilgrims' Steps leading up to the shrine, worn into ridges by the pilgrims' knees, and a shallow depression in the mosaic floor of Trinity Chapel, worn by pilgrims as they moved round the tomb.

Richard I (1189-1199)

Born in 1157; the eldest surviving son of Henry II; succeeded in 1189; died in 1199.

Richard was born at **Oxford,** in the palace of Beaumont. The site is marked by a small mean plaque on a pillar in Beaumont Street, opposite Worcester College.

His appalling character has been overlaid by his military reputation to make him Richard Lionheart, one of the earliest heroes of our childhood. Since he spent most of his reign abroad, on the Third Crusade in Palestine or in Austrian prisons, there is virtually nothing to remind us of him in Britain. He is buried at Fontevrault in France, though his heart is at Rouen. His wife, Berengaria of Navarre, who never even visited England, was buried at Epau in France, but in 1821 her tomb was moved to Le Mans Cathedral.

Some crusaders' tombs are to be seen in the **Temple Church** in London, though an effigy with crossed legs does not always imply a crusader. The equestrian statue of Richard in Old Palace Yard, **Westminster,** produced by Baron Marochetti in 1860, is a good example of Victorian medievalism and the perfect illustration of a child's idea of a crusader.

John (1199-1216)

Born in 1166 or 1167; youngest brother of Richard I; succeeded in 1199, ignoring the claim of his young nephew Prince Arthur; died in 1216.

Born in the palace of Beaumont, **Oxford,** John is one of the villains of English history, a tyrant, apparently without a redeeming feature. No attempt is ever made to whitewash him. His early life and reign are notable only because he plotted against his father Henry II, rebelled against his brother Richard I, lost most of England's French possessions and quarrelled with the Pope who, by 1213, had declared him excommunicated, then deposed. Thereafter the reign becomes spectacular.

John was compelled to submit to the Pope by surrendering his crown to the papal envoy and receiving it back in exchange for an annual tribute as a papal vassal. This humiliating little ceremony occurred at **Swingfield** or at **Temple Ewell,**

11

villages near Dover. The papal bull which ordered John's Irish vassals to renew their fealty to him is in the **Public Record Office Museum.** It bears an appropriately leaden seal.

By 1215 John had failed to form an anti-baronial party and, on 15th June 1215, 'in the meadow which is called **Runnymede** between Windsor and Staines' the barons forced him to seal a draft of Magna Carta. Blackstone, the great eighteenth-century lawyer, called Magna Carta 'the first ground and chief corner stone of the Common Law of England', yet no tangible memorial was raised to it until members of the American Bar Association set up a star-spangled dome over a pillar of English granite inscribed: 'To commemorate Magna Carta—Symbol of Freedom under the Law'. This stands on National Trust land at Runnymede and was dedicated as recently as 28th July 1957. We must realise, however, that the Great Charter was not the basis of liberty for the common man. No baron cared about him. The charter was framed to restrict the king's arbitrary prerogatives with a legal right of resistance and to extend the barons' power, and nothing more.

The name 'Magna Carta' refers to an idea rather than a single object. The document known as the Articles of the Barons, which was sealed at Runnymede, is in the **British Museum.** In the same showcase are two of the four surviving 'exemplifications' despatched over the king's seal. The other two copies are in the cathedral archives at **Lincoln** and **Salisbury.**

In October 1216 John was travelling from **King's Lynn** into Lincolnshire through **Wisbech,** a few miles south of the Wash. Although ill, he insisted on covering long distances every day and to save time the baggage train went by the direct but dangerous route across the 4½-mile wide estuary of the Nene between **Cross Keys** and **Long Sutton,** now silted and drained to provide firm ground. The traditional story is that the entire convoy, horses, men, treasure, holy relics and crown jewels, were all swept away by the tide or swallowed by the quicksands, leaving no survivors and a fantastic treasure trove that is still waiting to be found. More sober research suggests that only part of the convoy was overwhelmed and that anything of value was recovered at low water next day.

The disaster may have increased the king's illness but dysentery cannot have been helped by over-indulgence in peaches, fresh cider and possibly poisoned wine. John died in the castle of **Newark-on-Trent** in Nottinghamshire on 18th October 1216.

John was buried, as he desired, in **Worcester Cathedral,** before the high altar near the shrine of his patron saint, Wulfstan. The king's Purbeck marble effigy is the original coffin lid of about 1220 and the oldest royal effigy in England, though the carved tomb-chest on which it lies is fifteenth-century. The tomb was opened in 1797 and the king's body was found wrapped in a monk's cowl with well-preserved robes of crimson damask. Several items were removed as the exposed body turned to dust and are kept in a nearby case. They include his thumb-bone mounted in silver.

The many buildings named after King John usually have nothing to do with him. Just as earthworks and natural features were frequently named as the Devil's, so early stone buildings were attributed to the Jews or to King John. One authority lists thirteen such buildings of which only three or four are of the correct date. There is no proof that King John lived in any of them.

Henry III (1216-1272)

Born in 1207; elder son of King John; succeeded in 1216; died in 1272.

Henry III was born at **Winchester** and succeeded to the throne before his tenth birthday, with his father perhaps poisoned, his barons rebellious and his country invaded. He was therefore hastily crowned in the abbey church which is now **Gloucester Cathedral.** It is said that his mother's bracelet was used as a crown.

Henry particularly reverenced St. Edward the Confessor, who had been canonised in 1161. He spent much of his time rebuilding **Westminster Abbey** and providing the saint with a new, more magnificent shrine inside it. The work became so expensive that he had to pawn the jewels which he had given the shrine, jewels which had practically beggared him in the first place.

The end of his reign was less peaceful. His continual gifts of lands and offices to foreigners angered his barons so much that they made him accept the Provisions of Oxford in 1258. When he later rejected them, the barons chose Simon de Montfort as their leader and declared civil war. The choice was embarrassing, for Montfort was married to the king's sister Eleanor and his home was **Kenilworth Castle** (plate 16) in Warwickshire, England's greatest and most impregnable lake fortress.

The battle of **Lewes,** Sussex, was fought in 1264, ranging over the fields between Lewes and Offham, where the modern racecourse now stands. Henry's son, the future Edward I, marched out from Lewes Castle, attacked successfully and pursued his opponents for so long that Montfort had time to capture the king in his billet at St. Pancras Priory. There is a monument on Harry's Hill, Lewes.

During Henry's imprisonment by the baronial party, Prince Edward routed the barons at **Evesham** near Worcester in 1265 and killed Montfort. The battlefield is marked by a monument near the house called Abbey Manor, and we learn that eighteen barons were slain in the battle, 160 knights, and four thousand soldiers (plate 8).

Henry died seven years later and is buried in **Westminster Abbey** under a gilded bronze effigy of 1291. The purple porphyry slabs in his marble tomb-chest are said to have been brought back by Edward I after crusading in the Holy Land.

Edward I (1272-1307)

Born in 1239; elder son of Henry III; succeeded in 1272; died in 1307.

Edward I was born at **Westminster.** Although he is called the Hammer of the Scots and defeated them on more than one occasion, he never completely conquered them. The atmosphere of his reign is best sensed in North Wales where his ring of mighty castles formed both the emblem and the surety of Welsh subjection. **Harlech, Conway, Caernarvon** and **Beaumaris** are some of the most perfect specimens of medieval fortification in Britain and a visit to any of them demonstrates the power of a royal conqueror.

Caernarvon Castle is the best-known for it is the scene of the investiture of the Prince of Wales, but it is celebrated in its own right. It is almost intact and its Eagle Tower is among the largest single towers built in the Middle Ages. The castle, with its walls of coloured stone purposely built to resemble the Theodosian city walls of Constantinople, the quay, the town walls and gates took more than forty years to build and cost the equivalent of £2 million.

Edward was fully the man for such undertakings. ' Longshanks ' by name, he was 6 feet 2 inches tall, majestic and affable. In **Westminster Abbey** stands the Coronation Chair which encloses the Stone of Scone, the Stone of Destiny on which Scotland's kings were crowned and which he seized from them in 1296. He had the oak chair built to contain it in 1300-1 and every crowned monarch of this realm since Edward II, with one exception, has been crowned in the chair.

Edward's wife was the incomparable Eleanor of Castile. At her death in 1290 he brought her body from **Harby,** Nottinghamshire, to **Westminster** and at each of the twelve places where the procession rested for the night he erected a memorial, an Eleanor cross. One remains at **Geddington** in Northamptonshire, another at **Hardingstone,** Northamptonshire (plate 5), a third at **Waltham Cross** in Hertfordshire, but the best-known, in the forecourt of London's **Charing Cross** station, is a very free version built in the mid 1860s. The original stood a bow-shot away in the hamlet of Charing, called Cyrring before 1066 and so nothing to do with Eleanor the dear queen, *chère reine*. The cross stood where the statue of Charles I now stands (plate 15), halfway between the city of London and the city of Westminster. Parliament removed the cross in 1647 but Eleanor has a better memorial: the gilt bronze effigy under which she lies in **Westminster Abbey** is one of the finest in Europe.

As became a soldier, Edward died at the head of his troops, trying to conquer Scotland for the third time. His death occurred at **Burgh by Sands,** a village on the Cumbrian coast near Carlisle, and his body was brought to **Waltham Abbey** where it lay for several months before being placed in **Westminster Abbey.** His tomb is one of those surrounding the shrine of St. Edward the Confessor, after whom this Edward was named. It is a soldier's tomb, a completely plain chest formed of black Purbeck marble slabs. It was probably left unfinished at first because men expected Edward's wish to be fulfilled, that his bones should be carried before his army until Scotland was subdued. On one side of the tomb is a fittingly brief sixteenth-century inscription, now partly illegible and perhaps copying an earlier statement of this request: ' *Edwardus primus Scottorum malleus hic est. Pactum serva* '. (Here is Edward the first, hammer of the Scots. Keep the agreement).

Edward II (1307-1327)

Born in 1284; Edward I's fourth but eldest surviving son; succeeded in 1307; deposed and murdered in 1327.

Edward was born in the then unfinished **Caernarvon Castle,** which his father was building to subdue the Welsh. Alas for picturesque tradition, he was not created Prince of Wales until 1301 when he was seventeen and his presentation to the Welsh as a prince who was born in their land and spoke no English is not mentioned before 1584 when it was fashionable to flatter Elizabeth I's Welsh Tudor ancestry.

There are few to say anything good of his life which was foolish, frivolous and extravagant. A weakness for favourites like Piers Gaveston led to neglect of his royal duties and it was only a matter of time before he was deposed.

For a few months after his deposition, Edward was imprisoned in **Kenilworth Castle** and it was there that he abdicated the throne. He was next taken to **Berkeley Castle,** Gloucestershire, where his cell remains largely unaltered. Now outside the cell, but then in its corner, is a pit into which rotting animal carcases were thrown in the hope that their stench would suffocate or at least infect the prisoner. Every indignity and ill-treatment that might hasten the king's end was tried, but his constitution was strong enough to resist them all. At last it was thought necessary to murder him, by means quick but secret enough for his body to appear unblemished when exposed, so encouraging men to assume that his death was from natural causes. There are several rumours of the way in which Edward II was murdered and the most horrifically imaginative seems to be correct. Those who wish to impress others will recall with the medieval chroniclers that he was ' *cum veru ignito inter celanda confossus* '. The more squeamish will remember that his screams were heard outside the castle walls.

He was buried in **Gloucester Cathedral** under an idealised effigy and a brilliantly pinnacled canopy. The effigy is one of the finest extant fourteenth-century alabaster figures, carved at a time when alabaster was considered especially precious and so rarely used for such large works. Ironically, the tomb became a place of pilgrimage.

Edward III (1327-1377)

Born in 1312; elder son of Edward II; succeeded in 1327; died in 1377.

As a king who reigned for fifty years, Edward III is surprisingly difficult to represent intimately. He is the archetypal medieval king with a medieval king's virtues—capability, wisdom, mercy. His actions gave so much to England's heritage that they have become abstract, hard to see as the actions of one man.

During his reign, St. George was made the patron saint of England; we suffered the Black Death; Edward rebuilt **Windsor Castle,** where he was born; he founded the Order of the Garter at Windsor, fulfilling his vow to restore King Arthur's Round Table; his son was that epitome of medieval chivalry, the Black Prince; Geoffrey Chaucer lived during his reign, and John Wycliffe, 'the morning star of the Reformation'. Edward's claim through his mother to the French throne is seen as the start of the Hundred Years War and the reason why every king of England from Edward III to George III also called himself king of France. The most famous incident of the war almost certainly did happen, but seems straight out of chivalric legend—queen Philippa on her knees, begging her royal husband to have mercy on the six burghers of Calais, the nooses already round their necks. A copy of Rodin's statuary group is in the gardens beside the Houses of Parliament at **Westminster** and it is there that we come closer to Edward himself.

The official title of the Houses of Parliament is the New Palace of Westminster, but a few scraps of the original medieval royal palace remain on the site. One is the Jewel Tower in Old Palace Yard, the only surviving domestic part of the palace. It was built in 1365-6 at the palace's extreme south-west corner as a moated treasure-house for Edward III's private jewels, valuables and plate.

Nearby in **Westminster Abbey** are a shield and a double-handed sword, traditionally his. They stand by the Coronation Chair and the sword may be compared with his two-handed ceremonial sword, 6 feet 8¼ inches long, displayed in St. George's Chapel, **Windsor** (plate 7). Edward died at the palace of **Sheen** near Richmond, afterwards demolished by Richard II because his first wife died there. The beloved Philippa had died in 1369 and her alabaster figure is the oldest portrait effigy in **Westminster Abbey.** Edward's body was laid next to hers and along the Purbeck marble tomb are ranged little gilt bronze figures, portraits of six of their children, acting as 'weepers'.

Full-size effigies were originally made of wood, wax, or leather to be carried at the funerals of the great, and to lie in state, unlike later wax figures which were set up beside graves as eighteenth-century tourist attractions. In **Westminster Abbey Museum** is the head of Edward III's effigy, which may be the oldest wooden effigy of its type in Europe. The face is covered with a plaster and linen death mask, so well preserved that one can see the distortion, the flattened left cheek and the drooping mouth caused by the stroke from which he died.

The Black Prince

Born in 1330; eldest son of Edward III; died in 1376, a year before his father.

No record exists of the title 'Black Prince' before the sixteenth century but he was a legend in his own time and Edward Prince of Wales, England's darling, is one of the might-have-beens of English history. If he had survived his father, would England have been spared Richard II and the Peasants' Revolt? Would Bolingbroke have usurped the throne as Henry IV? Would there have been a Henry V or an Agincourt?

His title probably came from memories of his black armour, though his reputation was black enough in France where he spent much of his life on campaign. On the field of Crécy in 1346 he is said, traditionally but incorrectly, to have captured the ostrich-feather badge of the blind king of Bohemia and so introduced the 'Prince of Wales's feathers'. His motto *Ich dien* (I serve) also acted as his signature: the unique surviving example, dated 1370, is in the **Public Record Office Museum**—'*De par Homout Ich Dene*'.

Few tangible memories of his life remain. He was born at the now vanished palace of **Woodstock,** Oxfordshire. He married Joan, the Fair Maid of Kent, and there is a false tradition that they spent their honeymoon at Hall Place, **Bexley,** in south-east London, where part of the old building remains among lawns and trees and a set of Queen's Beasts in topiary. It was much extended in Tudor times. The late thirteenth-century manor-house called **Hellen's,** Much Marcle, near Ledbury, has a stone table at which the Black Prince dined.

The prince's tomb is in **Canterbury Cathedral** near the eastern end. His effigy follows the instructions he gave in his will: on the tomb 'we wish that an image covered in latten-brass shall be placed in memory of us, all armed in steel for battle with our arms quartered, and our face, with our leopard helmet placed beneath the head of our image'. The effigy lies ramrod straight, the hands in prayer, traces of the first gilding still visible. The tomb differs in one particular from his requirements: he wished to be buried in the Undercroft but

18

only a place of the utmost honour was thought worthy of such a prince. His tomb was placed in solitary glory near the shrine of St. Thomas Becket, the most sacred spot in England.

In a glass case nearby are the 'achievements' or 'hatchments' carried at his funeral in 1376 and perhaps used in tournaments: his helmet with a lion crest of moulded leather, a shield, a scabbard, gauntlets, and a surcoat embroidered with his coat of arms. Colourful reproductions hang on a beam over the tomb.

One more personal possession survives. The Black Prince sometimes fought in Spain and in 1367 Pedro the Cruel, king of Castile, gave him the huge stone which has ever since been called the Black Prince's Ruby. Henry V wore it in a circlet round his helm at Agincourt but now it forms a main jewel in the Imperial State Crown, one of the most splendid of the Crown Jewels to be seen in the new subterranean Jewel Chamber at the **Tower of London.**

Richard II (1377-1399)

Born in 1367; only surviving son of the Black Prince, and grandson of Edward III; succeeded in 1377; deposed in 1399; died in 1400.

We who are no longer involved with Richard of Bordeaux —where he was born—can admire him for his style. The gem-like painting called the Wilton Diptych which is in the **National Gallery** shows him supported by his patron saints, adoring the Virgin and Child. It was probably painted for him and even the angels wear his elegant badge, the white hart. He married the sister of that man so often supposed legendary, good king Wenceslas. He loved gold and jewels. On a lower level, his fastidiousness brought the handkerchief into England.

To his contemporaries his glacial hauteur and delicate behaviour appeared more like stubbornness, despotism and effeminacy. His one favourable action happened during the Peasants' Revolt of 1381. After Sir William Walworth had stabbed the peasants' leader Wat Tyler at **Smithfield,** now much changed from when it was one of London's large open spaces, a 'smooth field', the boy king really did go forward with amazing courage, shouting something like 'I will be your leader—follow me!', riding at the rabble's head until it could be controlled or dispersed. 'Walworth's dagger' is kept in **Fishmongers' Hall** by London Bridge and may occasionally be seen there. The attribution is untrue.

Richard II's career is best studied in Shakespeare's pageant of a play, but the sites of his downfall remain. He met Henry Bolingbroke, the future Henry IV, at **Flint Castle** in 1399 and virtually became his prisoner. According to Froissart, the king's favourite greyhound Mathe left him and fawned on the usurper, a nice sentimental touch. The castle stands on a low rock by the shore of the Dee estuary, Edward I's earliest castle in North Wales, but slighted by order of Parliament in 1647. Its bare walls and drum towers outline a castle plan unique in Britain, for the double-walled keep is outside the main castle square and connected to it by a drawbridge. Richard was brought from Flint to the **Tower of London**, deposed and sent as a prisoner to **Pontefract Castle** in Yorkshire which was also dismantled after the Civil War. Within a year he was dead, by violence or starvation. He was buried at **Kings Langley** in Hertfordshire, where there is a tomb richly decorated with many coats of arms and probably meant for him. In 1413 he was translated to lie among his royal ancestors in **Westminster Abbey.**

LANCASTER AND YORK

Henry IV (1399-1413)

Born in 1367; son of John of Gaunt, third surviving son of Edward III; king in 1399, usurping Richard II's throne; died in 1413.

Henry IV was born at **Bolingbroke Castle** in Lincolnshire, whence he took his surname. The enmity between him and Richard II began when Bolingbroke challenged the Duke of Norfolk who had accused him of treason. Richard banished them both and confiscated Henry's inheritance when John of Gaunt died.

Shortly afterwards Henry returned to England as an invader. He landed at the port of **Ravenspur,** one of several places on the coast of Humberside which have since been swallowed up by the sea. All that remains is a cross which may have stood in its market-place and is now in the grounds of Holyrood House, **Hedon,** Humberside. Henry drew up the charges against Richard in the castle at **Hertford,** a favourite royal residence for centuries though only a few oddments of its walls and towers remain.

The usurpation was successful but there were disaffected

men ready to take advantage of any difficulty. On 21st July 1403 the rebellious Henry Percy, known as Hotspur, was defeated and killed by Henry IV and Prince Hal, the future Henry V, at the battle of **Shrewsbury** in Salop. The church which stands on the battlefield was founded by the king as a chantry chapel to commemorate those who fell in the battle (plate 9).

It had been foretold that Henry would die in Jerusalem, a prophecy which had him continually preparing for a pilgrimage to the Holy Land which he never found the opportunity to make. Praying one day at the shrine of St. Edward the Confessor in **Westminster Abbey,** he suffered a fatal seizure and died shortly after being carried into a nearby room whose name derived from tapestries depicting incidents from the history of Jerusalem which once hung upon its walls. Then as now it was called the Jerusalem Chamber—or simply Jerusalem.

Henry and his queen Joan of Navarre are buried in a canopied tomb in **Canterbury Cathedral,** near the shrine of St. Thomas who might intercede for his complicity in the death of Richard II.

Henry V (1413-1422)

Born in 1387; eldest son of Henry IV; succeeded in 1413; died in 1422.

The idea of Henry V as England's hero king is largely a Shakespearian invention. Many English authorities and most French ones show us a less pleasant character.

Henry V was born at **Monmouth Castle** but the carved oak swinging cradle from Chepstow Castle in the **Museum of London** is his only by tradition, for it dates from no earlier than the fifteenth century. A few crumbling walls remain of the Norman castle at **Monmouth** but the town is still very proud of its famous son. There is a curiously awkward statue of him on the Guildhall and the central market-place is named Agincourt Square.

The change from riotous youth to sober young king is only partly based on fact for Prince Henry had worked strenuously in war and politics. As king he renewed Edward III's claim to the French throne and defeated the French in two campaigns, his greatest victory being Agincourt on 25th October 1415. His wars did not make him universally popular in England, however, and in the Lower High Street, **Southampton,** is the Red Lion Inn which incorporates Norman stonework and a fine medieval hall. This is traditionally the scene of the trial in 1415 of two peers who had conspired to assassinate the king in favour of a usurper.

After being declared heir to the French throne, Henry married Catherine of France, daughter of the mad king Charles VI. In two years he was dead of dysentery and his body was placed in a Purbeck marble tomb in **Westminster Abbey.** On top was an effigy covered by plates of silver gilt with a head of solid silver, but all this was stripped away by Henry VIII so that only the headless oaken core remained. A new head has recently been added. Addison made Sir Roger de Coverley suitably indignant about the obvious thief: ' Some Whig, I'll warrant you; you ought to lock up your kings better; they will carry off the body too, if you don't take care.' Perhaps greater treasures were saved: high on a beam above Henry V's chantry which is over the tomb are the king's ' hatchments', the shield, helmet and saddle which were carried at his funeral. In the **Westminster Abbey Museum** is a sword. Such objects were usually made especially for the funerals of medieval kings but there is the remotest possibility that these were actually used—at Agincourt.

Henry VI (1422-1461)

Born 6th December 1421; only son of Henry V; succeeded in 1422; crowned 6th November 1429; deposed 1461-70; restored 1470-1; murdered 1471.

Compelled to fill a post for which he had neither talent nor enthusiasm, Henry VI was bound to be a failure as king. His virtues increased his difficulties. A saintly patron of learning, honest, well-meaning, and ultimately a victim of the insanity which crazed his maternal grandfather, he was dominated by his wife, the ruthless Margaret of Anjou, ' the she-wolf of France'. Born at **Windsor Castle,** king of England at less than nine months old, king of France a few weeks later, he grew up to suffer inevitable comparison with his dead father, to be ignored or used as a puppet by his wife and the great magnates, and to be made a figurehead in the Wars of the Roses though he was the complete antithesis of a warrior king.

In more peaceful times he might have been a competent if not a great ruler. In 1440 he founded the school at **Eton,** 'The King's College of Our Lady of Eton beside Windsor', and in 1441 a sister college to receive its scholars, **King's College, Cambridge.** Despite many additions, the Lower

School at Eton dates from c. 1443 and is still in regular use while College Hall and the chapel, which was to be merely the choir of a much larger chapel, date from only a few years later. King's College was recently restored but has always been among the most beautiful colleges in Cambridge. Henry was far more than a nominal royal founder: the entire credit for these two institutions is his and they absorbed his whole interest.

He was dragged from such peaceful occupations into a civil war which, despite the popular idea of a mannered exercise in colourful chivalry, was an opportunity to settle old scores in a bloodbath. The Wars of the Roses ravaged the feudal families and provide one of the most acceptable points in our history for drawing a line to mark the end of the Middle Ages.

The war began in 1455 with the first battle of **St. Albans,** fought through the streets of that town and resulting in Henry's capture. Battle followed battle—**Blore Heath, Ludlow, Northampton, Wakefield, Mortimer's Cross** and the second battle of **St. Albans,** whereupon Edward Duke of York was declared king as Edward IV and Henry was deposed.

Sporadic fighting still occurred but it was not until the reconciliation of Queen Margaret and the Earl of Warwick that Edward's throne was shaken. Warwick betrayed Edward, invaded England in Henry's name, restored Henry to his throne and earned himself the title of 'the Kingmaker'. Only a few months passed before Edward IV proclaimed himself king once more and Warwick was defeated and killed at the battle of **Barnet** in 1471.

On 4th May 1471 the last battle of the Roses was fought at **Tewkesbury** in Gloucestershire. The site is south of the town and still called 'Bloody Meadow'. Henry and Margaret were captured but their son, Edward Prince of Wales, was killed and lies buried under the tower of the magnificent **Tewkesbury Abbey.** A modern brass plate marks the grave and the vaulted roof is set with gilded 'suns in splendour', the badge of Edward IV's triumphant House of York, placed there as tokens of his victory. Seventeen days later Henry VI was dead, officially found dead in bed 'of pure displeasure and melancholy', which is probably a polite description for murder. The body was buried at **Chertsey** in Surrey but translated to the new St. George's Chapel, **Windsor** (plate 7), in 1485. Henry was popularly venerated as a martyr, to such an extent that Henry VII hoped to have him canonised—

unsuccessfully. He lies under a plain stone slab, once the
site of many miracles. Beside the tomb hangs his original
iron alms-box, always used for pilgrims' offerings and marked
'H'.

Even if miracles and offerings belong to the past, Eton
remembers its founder still. The traditional site of his
murder is the deep recess on the east side of the former
Jewel Chamber in the Wakefield Tower of the **Tower of
London.** This was fitted up as a chapel and Henry is said
to have been murdered at prayer. On 21st May each year,
the anniversary of his death, the Eton authorities cover the
place with a sheaf of lilies and roses.

Edward IV (1461-1483)

*Born in 1441 or 1442; king in 1461 as rightful heir or
usurper; deposed 1470-1; restored 1471-83; died in 1483.*

Edward Duke of York first came to the throne at the
deposition of Henry VI after the battle of **Towton,** fought
on 29th March 1461 between Pontefract and Knaresborough
in North Yorkshire and known as the battle in the snow.
Warwick the Kingmaker lent his support to restore
Henry for a few months in 1470-71 but Edward regained
the throne by the battle fought at **Barnet** in Hertfordshire
on Easter Day, 14th April 1471, and known as the battle
in the fog. The battle of Barnet is commemorated by a
monument erected in 1740. This was not quite the end of
the Lancastrian cause. Edward defeated Henry's wife and
son in battle at **Tewkesbury** in 1471. He was safely king at
last.

Edward IV was born at Rouen. His grandfather was the
son of Edward III's fourth son, Edmund of Langley, but
his grandmother was descended from Edward III's second
son Lionel of Antwerp, which gave him a more senior
claim to the throne than Henry VI who was descended from
Edward III's third son, John of Gaunt. He was thought to
be a giant. He was 6 feet 3 or 4 inches tall, blond and
handsome. His affability and attempts to court popular
favour were appreciated but he was rarely able to conceal
the ruthless despotism of his rule and the scandalous excesses
of his private life.

One object stands in his defence and that is the result of
his jealousy. He was annoyed that Henry VI's chapel at
Eton must be in full view across the river from his castle at
Windsor, so in 1478 he began a rival. St. George's Chapel,

Windsor (plate 7), now the Garter Chapel and Edward's burial place, is among the finest pieces of Perpendicular architecture in Europe. Its magnificent stone vaulting was raised when the style was at the height of its development. This is one of the world's most beautiful places of worship.

Edward V (1483)

Born in 1470; eldest son of Edward IV; king from April to June 1483; afterwards he disappeared.

Edward is one of the puzzles of English history. He was the son of Edward IV, born at **Westminster**—but was he legitimate? He was king for 77 days in 1483 before his uncle Richard Duke of Gloucester was proclaimed king in his place for reasons which may be acceptable—Richard's birth and popularity could not be questioned, while the country did not want a child, even a legitimate child, as king. Young Edward came from his little court at **Ludlow Castle** to **Stony Stratford** on the Northamptonshire/Buckinghamshire border where he was met by his uncle and guardian Richard. From there he went to the **Tower of London,** a royal palace of the first rank and so a perfectly normal home for the young king. He was joined there by his younger brother Richard Duke of York and they were apparently never seen again.

At this point the legends began to grow. The supposed murderer of William Rufus had been a Tirel (see page 7) and it was said that one Sir James Tyrell had been hired by Richard III to kill the boys by smothering. They were thought to have been murdered in the Bloody Tower, so called from that deed, the assassins coming to them along the top of the wall now known as Raleigh's Walk. The crime traditionally happened in the little first floor room, dark, bare, and perhaps most memorable for the petty vandalism of visitors which means that its wooden walls show more scratched signatures than wall surface. Bones were found close by in 1674. They were thought to be those of the princes and in 1678 were buried by Charles II in an urn set near Elizabeth I's tomb in **Westminster Abbey.** Examination of the bones in 1933 suggested that they belonged to two brothers aged about ten and thirteen, of whom the elder may have been suffocated. Later research has partly discredited these findings, suggesting that the bones may not be those of boys, may come from much younger bodies and not necessarily from children who were suffocated. In short, it is probable that the bones are not those of the 'Little Princes in the Tower'.

What happened to the princes? Perhaps the Duke of Buckingham killed them. Perhaps Henry VII tidied them out of the way. Perhaps they just died at a time when such an announcement would have been embarrassing. At **Eastwell** in Kent there was an old man, a bricklayer who could read, a very rare accomplishment in 1545. Years earlier, he said, he had been taken before a man who claimed he was king of England but would be nothing if the Tudors won the next day's battle. The boy must stay silent if they did. One theory is that the boy was Richard's illegitimate son, but Richard had acknowledged others. Another theory is that he was Edward V, hiding from Henry VII and now Henry VIII. It is a good story.

The most immediate souvenir of the boy king is a slip of vellum in the **British Museum**. About the size of a postcard, it was cut from a book and must date from those 77 days in 1483. It bears three autograph inscriptions, almost as if it were from a child's collection:

> *R(ex) Edwardus quintus*
> *Loyaulte me lie. Richard Gloucestre*
> *Souente me souenne. Harre Bokyngham*

Richard III (1483-1485)

Born in 1450; youngest brother of Edward IV; king by acclamation in 1483; killed in battle in 1485.

The widely held opinion that Richard III was a monstrous tyrant, deformed, and a murderer, is based on Shakespeare's play, a political work written during the reign of Elizabeth I. Richard had been overthrown by Elizabeth's grandfather, the usurper Henry Tudor, and the play was based on books written by Henry's supporters. It is known that Richard had been extremely popular as Duke of Gloucester and was greatly mourned at his death, particularly in the North. He had been made king by acclamation, whereas for Henry VII to be safely enthroned the Princes in the Tower had to be dead. It is arguments like these that lead many people to see Richard III as the victim of a remarkably successful Tudor campaign to blacken his reputation.

Richard was born at **Fotheringhay Castle** in Northampton-shire, though the castle was pulled down in 1627 and only its mound remains, the river Nene winding at its foot. In the nearby church are monuments erected by Elizabeth I to Richard's parents, Richard Duke of York and Cecily Neville, and to his young brother, Edmund Earl of Rutland, killed with their father in 1460 at the battle of **Wakefield.**

Edward IV made his brother Lord of the North with complete control of England north of the Trent. Richard moved round the country from York to Pontefract to Carlisle but usually resided at his favourite castle, **Middleham** in Wensleydale. This was the 'Windsor of the North' where the Nevilles had lived in almost royal state until they were disgraced at the Kingmaker's fall. Richard married Anne Neville and obtained the castle. It was already decayed when Cromwell slighted it but one may still climb to the top of its Norman keep where it stands on a high slope above the river Ure.

During mid 1483 Richard was staying at **Crosby Hall,** at that time in London's Bishopsgate, and there is a strong tradition that he was offered the crown there. In 1910 the hall was re-erected in Cheyne Walk, **Chelsea,** on part of Sir Thomas More's garden, and there we may visit it for its associations and its fine hammerbeam roof.

In the same year Richard stayed at the Angel Inn in the High Street at **Grantham,** Lincolnshire. Despite late eighteenth-century additions and a new name, the Angel and Royal Hotel, part of the building is fourteenth-century, which makes it one of the oldest inns in the country. King John is even said to have held court there in 1213. Its fifteenth-century stone front faces the market square and a celebrated oriel window springs from an angel corbel. The 'King's Room' is still pointed out, for Richard signed the Duke of Buckingham's death warrant here on 19th October 1483.

The night before the battle of Bosworth, Richard stayed at the Blue Boar Inn, **Leicester.** This was demolished last century, but is remembered by Blue Boar Lane off Highcross Street. He rode out to the battle across the old Bow Bridge. This was rebuilt last century but a metal plaque repeats the tradition that Richard's spur knocked the bridge parapet as he left the town and a wise woman foretold that his head would hit the same stone on his return. Betrayed and defeated, his dead body was thrown over a horse, brought back across Bow Bridge and, of course, his head banged against the same stone. He was buried without honour in the church of the Greyfriars, Leicester, but at the Dissolution of the monasteries his bones were thrown into the neighbouring river Soar. It is not clear whether they remained there or were recovered and buried near Bow Bridge.

Ambien Farm, south of **Market Bosworth,** was the centre of the battle and one may see King Richard's Well near which he is said to have died. The battle ranged over the slopes of Ambien Hill and, in the church at **Sutton Cheney,** a brass plate has been erected by the Richard III Society, a group dedicated to clearing his name.

THE TUDORS

Henry VII (1485-1509)

Born in 1455 or 1457; only son of Edmund Tudor (son of Catherine, widow of Henry V, and Owen Tudor, the Clerk of her Wardrobe); king by conquest in 1485; died in 1509.

Henry was a Tudor, a Welsh nobleman, born in **Pembroke Castle,** whose claim to the throne could only be by conquest and by marriage with Edward IV's daughter, the Yorkist heiress Elizabeth. He slandered Richard III, executed the Duke of Clarence's son who had a fairly good claim to the throne, and may even have murdered the Princes in the Tower.

The tradition that gives Henry VII a crown plucked from a thorn-bush after the battle of **Bosworth** rarely shows him as having the mind, however efficient, of a clerk. He created a new society but it was one to support him and from which he could extort money. He encouraged peace and trade probably because they were cheaper than war. One of his more endearing habits was to check and initial every receipt issued by the Treasurer of the King's Chamber. A book of these receipts is displayed in the **Public Record Office Museum,** each entry personally subscribed ' H '. His queen also checked and signed every page of the book listing her income and private expenses, so we cannot be surprised that Henry was one of the richest kings in Europe and died a millionaire. Few of his personal possessions survive but his autographed prayer-book is at **Chatsworth,** Derbyshire. His portrait dated 1505 in the **National Portrait Gallery** is the earliest of an English king definitely painted from life.

When Elizabeth of York died, she lay in state in St. John's Chapel in the **Tower of London** with eight hundred tapers burning round her bier. The head of her funeral effigy is with

Henry's, taken from his death mask, in **Westminster Abbey Museum:** they are two of the finest in the collection and close by is the tomb for which we can perhaps forgive Henry all his other faults—his greed, his avarice, his cunning. Henry VII's Chapel forms the east end of **Westminster Abbey** and its decoration, especially its fan vaulting, reaches unparalleled heights of splendour. The royal tomb is the masterpiece of Pietro Torrigiani of Florence, whose fist broke Michelangelo's nose. Gilt bronze effigies of Henry and Elizabeth lie on a sarcophagus of black and white marble, surrounded by an amazingly intricate bronze grille. This royal mausoleum has justifiably been called 'the most beautiful chapel in all Christendom'.

Arthur, Prince of Wales

Born in 1486; elder son of Henry VII; died in 1502, before his father.

Henry VII's elder son was born in **Winchester** and baptised in the cathedral there. Seen as a symbolic figure for a new country, the fruit of union between the red rose of Lancaster and the white rose of York, the hope of a new world of peace and learning, he was specifically named after the legendary champion of England.

In 1501, at the age of fifteen and after negotiations lasting thirteen years, he was married to Catherine of Aragon, the daughter of Ferdinand and Isabella of Spain, the patrons of Columbus. They commemorated the betrothal by presenting Henry VII with a stained glass window now in **St. Margaret's, Westminster,** the church beside Westminster Abbey. The gorgeous fifteenth-century stained glass preserved in **Great Malvern** priory church, near Worcester, includes a contemporary portrait of Prince Arthur kneeling at prayer. The **British Museum** occasionally displays a love-letter written in Latin by Arthur to Catherine before they were married. It is dated 1st November 1499 and begins with the delightfully stilted 'Most illustrious and excellent lady, our dearest Betrothed . . . ' Arthur was just thirteen.

The letter was written from the prince's castle at **Ludlow** in Salop, and it was there that he took his new bride. Ludlow was a magnificent border castle, a principal garrison in the chain of fortresses from Chepstow to Chester. Only the bare walls remain today but one especially admires the round chapel tower dating from the twelfth century.

After five months of marriage, Arthur died. His funeral

took place on 25th April 1502 and he was laid in a granite tomb in a chantry chapel erected to his memory in **Worcester Cathedral**. Badly mutilated by Edward VI's commissioners, its rich carving can still be identified, saints and apostles, coats of arms, Tudor badges, the Prince of Wales's feathers, the Garter, portcullises and roses, falcons and fetterlocks. It was little enough to commemorate the greatest hope of the new Tudor dynasty. He was fifteen years old.

Henry VIII (1509-1547)

Born in 1491; only surviving son of Henry VII; succeeded in 1509; died in 1547.

Henry VIII was meant to be Archbishop of Canterbury. His father Henry VII had united the warring factions of York and Lancaster by marrying Elizabeth of York. The first son was called Arthur and expected to become king. Henry VII saw how useful it would be if the king's brother were head of the church, so the young Henry was trained in theology and church music. Later he remembered enough to write an attack on Luther which won him the papal title *Fidei Defensor*, Defender of the Faith, a legend still appearing on our coins. Arthur's death overthrew the plan. Henry would be king.

It is easy to become confused about Henry. On one side he is the satyr with six wives, the autocrat who suppressed the monasteries, created a nobility of time-servers, and tried to blackmail the conscientious with judicial murder. On the other he is, as a young man, the 'undoubted flower and heir' of two reconciled dynasties, a fine musician, scholar, linguist and athlete; as an older man, he is Bluff King Hal, the embodiment of roast beef and Merrie England. Perhaps we may trace the man and avoid the moral judgements.

He was born at **Greenwich,** unfortunately for us in the rambling medieval palace demolished by Charles II in about 1660. He was baptised in the old church at Greenwich, also long demolished. Greenwich must have resembled **Hampton Court** (plate 12), begun by Cardinal Wolsey but in 1529 taken over by Henry as a royal palace. Although built in Tudor times, the remaining Tudor parts show that Hampton Court was an old-fashioned medieval-style building with some Renaissance detail stuck on to the rose-red brick. The Great Hall was built for Henry, together with the Real Tennis Court. This is the oldest tennis court still in use and even the most casual observer can see how far the game differs from mere lawn tennis. Henry's private apartments were destroyed by Sir Christopher Wren when he rebuilt one side of the palace in the seventeenth century, but it is not difficult to visualise Henry spending his honeymoons here with Anne Boleyn, Catherine Howard and Catherine Parr.

Despite such matters, Henry managed to get out now and again. He is known to have visited **Compton Wynyates** in Warwickshire, the home of his boyhood friend Sir William Compton and the most attractive early Tudor house in Britain. He visited **Winchester** with the Emperor Charles V and it was for that occasion that the round table on the west wall of Winchester Castle's Great Hall was painted or repainted with the Tudor Rose, a portrait of King Arthur and the names of the Knights of the Round Table.

A surprising number of personal items associated with Henry VIII have survived. His boxwood rosary with beads carved after designs by the court painter Holbein is at **Chatsworth.** His prayer-book, bearing his signature and that of his daughter Mary, is at **Elton Hall,** Cambridgeshire. The bull which Pope Clement VII issued in 1524 to confirm the royal title *Fidei Defensor* is displayed, complete with its golden seal, in the **Public Record Office Museum,** London. At **Windsor Castle** is the splendid series of Holbein drawings of Henry's courtiers and it is among them that we are perhaps closest to him.

Other relics are more military. In the White Tower of the **Tower of London** are kept the suits of armour made for the slim young Henry in 1515. The suits of 1520 and 1540 were made by the celebrated royal armourers of Greenwich but cannot disguise a swelling rotundity. His last extant armour also dates from about 1540 and stands at the head of the Grand Staircase in **Windsor Castle.** It shows him as hugely corpulent, probably the victim of a glandular disease —during one period of five years his armour suggests that his waist measurement increased by seventeen inches.

Henry lies in a vault marked by a simple marble slab in the choir of St. George's Chapel, **Windsor.** On its last journey from Westminster to Windsor, Henry's body lay for one night at Syon Abbey, later to become the magnificent **Syon House,** but then thought of as the sole English convent of the Bridgettine order and suppressed by the king. What happened was interpreted as heaven's answer to the desecration: in 1535 it had been prophesied 'that God's judgements were ready to fall upon his head . . . and that the dogs would lick his blood as they had done Ahab's.' The metaphorical became the physical. During the night the coffin burst open and dogs were found licking up remains from the floor.

The wives of Henry VIII

1. CATHERINE OF ARAGON
Born 1485; married Henry 1509; marriage annulled 1533; died 1536.

It would have broken the Spanish alliance and Henry VII's frugal heart to return Catherine's immense dowry to Spain at Arthur's death. The following year he betrothed her to his second son Henry and, a fortnight after his father's death in 1509, Henry VIII married her.

From those earlier, happier years we have three relics. St. Botolph's, **Lullingstone,** Kent, is a miniature church actually standing on the lawn of the great house next door. Inside is a carved oak screen. Sir John Peche, lord of the manor in the early sixteenth century, was a distinguished member of Henry VIII's court and he copied the screen from Henry VII's tomb, adding peach stones for his name and Catherine's pomegranate badge. Beside the high altar in St. George's Chapel, **Windsor,** is the Royal Closet, a heavily carved wooden oriel window, very like a theatre box. Henry placed it there to give Queen Catherine a secluded view of the Garter ceremonies. It was later used by Queen Victoria, in retirement after Prince Albert's death, to attend joyful occasions like royal weddings without appearing in public. Catherine must have attended service with the psalter she inherited from her mother-in-law, Elizabeth of York. It contains both their autograph inscriptions of ownership and they scribbled family notes into the calendar: it includes the only evidence known for Prince Arthur's day of birth. The book belongs to Exeter College, **Oxford,** but is displayed in the Divinity School there.

The whirlwind romances of an ageing royal Bluebeard often make us forget that Henry VIII and his first wife were married for no less than twenty-four years and had at least six children. One girl, the future Queen Mary, survived. The rest were still-born or died in infancy. Henry's entirely laudable wish to continue the Tudor dynasty with a legitimate

1. *King Arthur and his queen, Guinevere, are reputedly buried at Glastonbury Abbey in Somerset.*

2. *The Rufus Stone in the New Forest marks the probable spot where William II was killed by an arrow while hunting.*

3. *Reading Abbey is the burial place of Henry I, its founder, and became one of the most powerful of English abbeys.*

4. *Rosamund's Well in Blenheim Park, Oxfordshire, is named after Henry II's mistress who lived in the now vanished Woodstock palace.*

5. *The Eleanor cross at Hardingstone, Northamptonshire, is one of the three surviving crosses erected by Edward I to mark the resting places of his queen's body.*

6. Berkhamsted Castle, Hertfordshire, where William the Conqueror received the submission of England.

7. St George's Chapel, Windsor, the burial place of many kings and queens, was begun in 1478 by Edward IV as a rival to Henry VI's chapel at Eton.

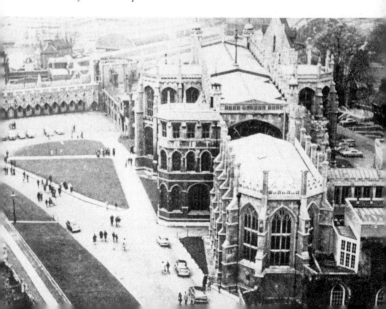

8. This monument marks the site of the battle of Evesham in 1265, in which Prince Edward defeated the barons, whose leader Simon de Montfort was slain.

9. The church on the battlefield of Shrewsbury was built by Henry IV to commemorate those killed in his defeat of Hotspur's rebels (1403).

10. *St James's Palace, Westminster, was the birthplace of Charles II, James II, Mary II, Queen Anne and George IV.*

11. *Hever Castle, Kent, was the family home of Anne Boleyn, and here she was courted by Henry VIII.*

12. Hampton Court was started by Cardinal Wolsey, but was taken over by Henry VIII in 1529, and became one of his chief palaces.

13. Catherine Parr, Henry VIII's sixth wife and widow, later married Lord Seymour, at whose home, Sudeley Castle, she died and is buried.

14. The cross at Ampthill marks the site of the castle where Catherine of Aragon lived for a while after her divorce from Henry VIII.

15. The statue of Charles I at Charing Cross, cast in 1633, stands on the site of the original Eleanor cross.

16. *Kenilworth Castle, slighted in the Civil War, was where, in 1575, Elizabeth I was entertained by her favourite, Robert Dudley, Earl of Leicester.*

17. *Bonnie Prince Charlie held court in the Palace of Holyroodhouse in Edinburgh after his victory at Prestonpans in 1745.*

18. *From King Charles's Tower, on the walls of Chester, Charles I is said to have watched his army defeated at the battle of Rowton Heath.*

19. *The former George Inn, Bridport, where the disguised Charles II stayed, and narrowly avoided recognition, during his escape from Worcester in 1651.*

20. *After the battle of Worcester Charles II fled to Boscobel House, Shropshire, where he hid in an oak tree.*

21. *The statue of William III on Brixham quay where he landed on 5th November 1688.*

22. *Kew Palace, in the seventeenth-century Dutch style, was the favourite residence of George III and his family.*

23. *Louis XVIII of France, brother of the guillotined Louis XVI, lived in exile at Hartwell House near Aylesbury from 1807 to 1814.*

24. *At Bushy House near Hampton Court the Duke of Clarence, later to become William IV, lived with his mistress, Mrs Jordan.*

25. *The royal mausoleum at Frogmore, Windsor, is the burial place of Queen Victoria, of her husband, Prince Albert, and of Edward VIII.*

male heir nourished his idea that the dead babies were God's curse on him, a direct sign that the papal dispensation had been insufficient—he should never have married his brother's widow and would never beget a legitimate son until she was put away. For reasons of his own safety as well as politics, the pope would not annul the marriage so Henry made himself head of the church in England and annulled it personally.

For the years between the annulment in 1533 and her death in 1536, Catherine bore her undeserved misfortune with courage, forbearance and prayer. She always insisted that she was Henry's wife and queen, as indeed she was in the eyes of most of Europe. In the park at **Ampthill,** Bedfordshire, is a cross bearing a shield with the arms of Castile and Aragon, which marks the site of Ampthill Castle where she stayed for part of this time (plate 14). She also found refuge in **Buckden Palace,** Cambridgeshire, the palace of the Bishops of Lincoln since the twelfth century. There she lived entirely in one room, overcome with misery, always fearing poison. She moved lastly to **Kimbolton Castle,** also in Cambridgeshire, a Tudor mansion since remodelled by Vanbrugh and Adam. There she died.

Her body was taken to **Peterborough Cathedral,** perhaps more famous for its curious wooden ceiling painted in about 1220, and although her tomb was destroyed in 1643 her remains lie there still. An infanta of Spain may deserve a rich or gaudy monument, but for a lady of such spirit and strength of mind as Catherine, her memorial is entirely fitting: a plain grey stone in the north choir aisle, flanked by the standards of sixteenth-century England and Spain.

2. ANNE BOLEYN

Born 1507(?); married Henry 1533; executed 1536.

Anne Boleyn—or, less poetically, Bullen—had many chances of recognition by King Henry. Her grandfather had been a leading minister, her father was in the royal favour, and her sister Mary was the king's mistress. Henry saw her and became infatuated, indeed the closing stages of the ' King's Great Matter ', the divorce from Catherine of Aragon, were completed at such dizzy speed because Anne was already expecting Henry's child and it must be born legitimate. The child was a girl.

Henry could not know that the child was destined to be Elizabeth I. Anne had failed him and must pay. The dark eyes and black hair were forgotten. Henry remembered her sixth finger and her witch's mole. Their days of courtship at her family home, the moated late thirteenth-century **Hever Castle** in Kent (plate 11), were past. Now she was held prisoner in a small room in the King's House within the **Tower of London,** today the residence of its Governor and so well preserved that it looks absurdly modern. Her father, Sir Thomas, became Earl of Wiltshire and was buried in St. Peter's church, **Hever,** under an effigy wearing full Garter robes. Anne was beheaded with a sword on **Tower Green** and buried in the Tower chapel of St. Peter ad Vincula in an elm chest made for arrows. There is little warmth in the tradition that sympathisers buried her heart in the church at **Ewarton** in Suffolk, though a heart-shaped casket was found in its chancel wall in 1836.

Henry's charge against her was adultery, probably overstated but not unfounded. Nevertheless he had once adored her and his love-letters show it, 'written with the hand of him that was, is, and shall be yours by his will H(enricus) R(ex)'. They may reasonably be described as torrid—they are preserved in the chaste presses of the Vatican Library!

3. JANE SEYMOUR
Born 1509; married Henry 1536; died 1537.

She was probably born in her father's home, **Wolfhall,** Savernake in Wiltshire, while an unlikely tradition asserts that she married Henry VIII in the Great Barn there. This was used as a quarry after the Civil War and only a few stones remain.

Her shrouded ghost holds a flickering candle as it walks through the corridors of **Hampton Court** to the room, long ago demolished, where Queen Anne Boleyn found her in Henry's arms. She was betrothed to the king on the day after Anne's execution and married him a week later. A fortnight after giving birth to Henry's long-awaited male heir, the future Edward VI, she died of puerperal fever.

Henry chose Jane Seymour to share his tomb in St. George's Chapel, **Windsor.** It is not clear whether this was because she was the mother of his son or because she died before he had time to grow tired of her.

4. ANNE OF CLEVES
Born 1515; married Henry 1540; marriage annulled 1540; died 1557.

Henry VIII married her for political reasons. She was

ill-equipped to be his queen but this was a minor point if she had also been imported for breeding a son and so 'was no better than a Flanders mare'. The political scene rapidly changed and, although unable to avoid the marriage, he had it annulled as quickly as possible and they parted almost by consent, Anne acquiescing in all that the king wished. She took the title of 'king's sister' and lived on in England in retirement, first at **Richmond** and **Bletchingley** in Surrey, though little now remains, afterwards at **Chelsea** where she died. She is buried in **Westminster Abbey.**

5. CATHERINE HOWARD
Born (?); married Henry 1540; executed 1542.

She married Henry at **Oatlands,** his vanished royal palace near Weybridge in Surrey. Eighteen months later she was executed on **Tower Green** for infidelity and was buried in the Tower chapel of St. Peter ad Vincula.

Her ghost has been seen in the Haunted Gallery at **Hampton Court** re-enacting the day when she escaped her guards and tried to reach the king her husband to plead for mercy. She was seized near the Chapel Royal where he was attending mass and was carried back shrieking to her room.

6. CATHERINE PARR
Born 1512; married Henry 1543; died 1548.

She was born in the now ruined Norman castle at **Kendal** in Cumbria. Her silver-bound book of devotions is kept in the town hall there.

Her marriage to Henry was celebrated at **Hampton Court** and was what a more modern age would call sophisticated: she was his sixth wife, he was her third husband and she survived him long enough to marry a fourth. The most attractive thing we know of her was the kindness she showed her stepchildren, Edward, Mary and Elizabeth, who can have had little affection during their infancy or adolescence and not much afterwards.

The **British Museum** displays a book of prayers written by Queen Catherine Parr, but translated into Latin, French and Italian and copied out by the future queen Elizabeth, for presentation to her father Henry VIII, apparently as a New Year's gift.

Catherine's fourth husband was Lord Seymour of Sudeley and it was in **Sudeley Castle,** Gloucestershire (plate 13), that she died. She is buried in the chapel there which dates from about 1460. The castle was dismantled after the Civil War but partly rebuilt last century. There can be few private houses in the world which enclose the grave of a queen.

Edward VI (1547-1553)

Born in 1537; son of Jane Seymour and Henry VIII; succeeded in 1547; died in 1553.

The only legitimate son of Henry VIII, Edward succeeded to the throne at the age of nine and died of rapid consumption before he was sixteen. Born at **Hampton Court,** he died at **Greenwich,** and it is more than likely that, had he survived, this puny sickly youth would have been a greater tyrant than his sister Bloody Mary. Religion can be dangerous in excess and Edward was a Protestant zealot.

We cannot get close to him. His nurse Mrs. Sibel Penn, known as ' Mother Jack ', is buried in **Hampton Church** by Hampton Court. In the **Oxford Divinity School** is a page from his copybook dated 16th February 1548, with his Latin sentences and phrases neatly begun, less neatly completed. The **British Museum** has part of his diary and a much corrected essay he wrote at twelve on the Sacrament of the Body and Blood of Christ: his tutor's comments are interlined.

The **National Portrait Gallery** has a portrait of him in perspective. This means that it is totally out of proportion from the front and recognisable only when squinted at through a spy-hole at the side.

He is buried in **Westminster Abbey.**

Lady Jane Grey

Born in 1537; executed 1554.

The daughter of Frances Duchess of Suffolk, who was the daughter of Princess Mary of England, a sister of Henry VIII, Lady Jane Grey thus had a claim to the throne, but one that was junior to that of Henry VIII's daughters Mary and Elizabeth, and to that of the Scots royal house who were descended from an elder sister of Henry VIII called Margaret.

She was one of the most captivating characters in a fearsome time, a valuable pawn in the hands of others. In **Bradgate Park,** Newton Linford, north-west of Leicester, is the home of the Greys, with the early Tudor red-brick ruins now partly rebuilt. Jane was born here, growing up with rank and beauty, her intellectual gifts well tutored, an ideal childhood for one who preferred reading Plato in Greek to hunting in her father's park.

Unfortunately she was a great-niece of Henry VIII and also a Protestant. On these grounds Protector Northumberland persuaded the dying Edward VI to 'devise' the throne away from Princess Mary, the rightful but Roman Catholic heiress, and towards Lady Jane Grey who was married to Guildford Dudley, Northumberland's son. The sixteen-year-old Jane was unwilling to usurp the throne but was at last forced to it, doing what she was told but absolutely against her own will. She accepted the crown at her father-in-law's home, **Syon House,** where the barrack-like walls mask a sumptuous interior decorated for a later Duke of Northumberland by Robert Adam.

Jane was proclaimed queen but the country supported Mary: in the **British Museum** is a letter seeking allegiance signed 'Jane the Quene' and another is in the **Public Record Office Museum.** She reigned for nine days in July 1553 and was then taken to the **Tower of London** where she was lodged in the Yeoman Gaoler's House, overlooking Tower Green. Her husband was in the Beauchamp Tower and on its wall may be seen the word IANE, supposedly scratched by him. She saw Guildford go out to his execution on Tower Hill and an hour later she saw his headless body brought back in a cart. She was executed on the same day. Their bodies lie together in the Tower chapel of St. Peter ad Vincula.

Mary I (1553-1558)

Born in 1516; daughter of Henry VIII and Catherine of Aragon; succeeded her brother Edward VI in 1553; died in 1558.

It was Mary's misfortune to be a completely sincere woman. Shamefully treated by her father, even bastardised to permit his marriage with Anne Boleyn, she turned for comfort to her Roman Catholic religion as became the daughter of Catherine of Aragon. Her lonely, unhappy, embittered childhood made her a religious fanatic, concerned only with reversing what she saw as her father's great sin and bringing England back to the path of her true faith.

Mary was born in the vanished **Greenwich Palace** but spent much of her childhood at **Hunsdon** near Harlow in Essex, a property bought by Henry VIII as a house for his children. Though much changed, its walls are still of Tudor brick. As Edward VI lay dying, Mary heard that support was growing for the Protestant Lady Jane Grey. Sending letters to the Council of State claiming the throne, she fled from Hunsdon to **Framlingham Castle** in Suffolk, where she was secure from surprise attack and nearer the sea if escape became necessary. Ruins of the late twelfth-century castle remain. During Mary's visit it was owned by the Roman Catholic Howard family. One of them was Thomas, third Duke of Norfolk, uncle to both Anne Boleyn and Catherine Howard, and the man who survived the block only because Henry VIII died on the eve of his execution by attainder.

For three weeks during July 1553 Mary stayed in the castle while her supporters gathered and she did not move until she had been proclaimed queen and Jane Grey was a prisoner. Now Mary could bring her country back to Rome, a task she began by marrying the country main marriageable champion of Roman Catholicism in Europe, the future Philip II of Spain. In 1554 she was betrothed to his proxy, Count Egmont, in St. John's Chapel in the **Tower of London.** The Spanish ambassador's gift on that occasion was a gold and crystal posset set attributed to Benvenuto Cellini which remains one of the most important treasures to be seen in **Hatfield House.** At **Castle Ashby** in Northamptonshire is the Moro portrait of Mary that she sent to her future husband. On 25th July 1554 Bishop Gardiner married Mary and Philip in **Winchester Cathedral.** The chair she sat in during the ceremony is kept in Bishop Gardiner's Chantry in the cathedral.

Philip rapidly tired of his plain and prematurely aged wife, soon returning to Spain and leaving Mary to earn a reputation for being hated unequalled in this country's history. Convinced that she was right, she knew she must compel the body if it saved the soul. Her devotion and her marriage with a Spaniard had made her passively unpopular, the subject of the nursery rhyme ' Mary, Mary, quite contrary ', but she now began a religious persecution, burning about three hundred Protestants, which not only caused a revulsion against Rome of which traces still linger in Britain but also earned her the name ' Bloody Mary '.

In 1849 excavations at London's **Smithfield** in the road beside St. Bartholomew's Hospital revealed charred oak posts, a staple and a ring, all surrounded with ashes and human remains. This was undoubtedly the spot where the forty-three Smithfield martyrs were burned at the stake and, on the wall of ' Barts ', the Protestant Alliance set up a dull little memorial to three of them. Its pink and black marble is made memorable by a single master stroke: the black iron railings before the tablet are topped with gilded five-fold spikes. The flames burn still.

It seems doubtful whether Mary appreciated her people's reaction to such deeds. Her famous lament concerns neither unpopularity nor religion but her loss of Calais, our last possession in France. She died unmourned and was buried in **Westminster Abbey** where she lies in the tomb of her golden sister Elizabeth. Obviously Mary damaged her religion irreparably and it is fitting that, between her death and the building of Elizabeth's tomb forty or so years later, her only memorial was the debris from the broken altars in Henry VII's Chapel heaped over the place where she lay buried.

Elizabeth I (1558-1603)

Born in 1533; daughter of Henry VIII and Anne Boleyn; succeeded her sister Mary in 1558; died in 1603.

How can one summarise 'the mirror of her sex and age', the queen who gave her name to the most magnificent and colourful reign in English history, a time when England became a naval power and Spanish sea-might was broken, the era of Shakespeare and Sidney, Raleigh and Drake? Dazzled by her later years, we would profit from studying her youth.

She was born at **Greenwich** though the only relics of her there are in St. Alfege's church. They are two organ keyboards on which the young Elizabeth is said to have played when Thomas Tallis was organist in the church which preceded the fine Classical building we visit today.

Her name is more closely linked with **Hatfield House** in Hertfordshire, but we must remember that she never saw the present house. It was the old fifteenth-century Hatfield that formed her principal residence from when she was three months old until her accession, and much of the time she was virtually a prisoner. Indeed on Palm Sunday 1554 she began two months' confinement in the Bell Tower of the **Tower of London** because she was thought to be implicated in Wyatt's rebellion against Mary's marriage with Philip of Spain. She refused to enter the Tower by Traitors' Gate, and sat on a stone in the Thames mud, crying 'Better sit here than in a worse place'. A section of the rampart where she was allowed exercise is still called Elizabeth's Walk.

She returned to **Hatfield** after her release and it was while sitting under an oak tree in the park there that she heard of her accession to the throne. She held her first council in the Great Hall which is the only part of the old house remaining and it seems appropriate that the ancient eating place should now be the visitors' restaurant. Beside it is the early seventeenth-century house, the present Hatfield, full of transplanted memories. There is the 'Rainbow Portrait' by Zuccharo, showing her dress covered with eyes and ears because she saw all and heard all that happened in her realm. There are the letters she wrote as a girl, the beautiful italic script contrasting with the violent and illegible 'skrating' hand for which she always apologised in her old age. It can be seen in a letter to her successor, James VI of Scotland, which is preserved in the **British Museum.** In the 180-foot Long Gallery at **Hatfield** are her most immediate relics—her gloves, her openwork garden hat, and the frilly-topped knitted silk stockings said to be the first pair in England. On the staircase is a portrait of the white horse she rode to review her troops at **Tilbury** when the Spanish Armada was imminent and she spoke of having the heart and stomach of a king. Elsewhere in the house is a saddlecloth, possibly the one she used that day. Another saddle said to be hers and in the Tudor colours, green and silver, is kept with her pocket handkerchief in the Great Hall of **Warwick Castle.**

Near Warwick is another castle, **Kenilworth** (plate 16), slighted in the Civil War by having a wall blown out so that it would be useless for further defence against the Roundheads. The brownish-pink walls do little to remind us that here in July 1575 Elizabeth was entertained for nineteen days by her favourite Robert Dudley, Earl of Leicester. It is all described in Sir Walter Scott's novel.

Elizabeth loved to travel through her kingdom which means that many houses can truthfully boast the old chestnut ' Queen Elizabeth slept here'. At **Wilton,** the home of the Earl of Pembroke, near Salisbury, is a lock of her hair which she gave to Sir Philip Sidney during a visit in 1583. **Cowdray Park** in Sussex is now known for its polo matches but, preserved among the ruins of the old mansion, are the banqueting hall and state bedchamber where Elizabeth slept in 1591. She stayed at **Loseley Park,** near Guildford in Surrey, three times. The owner has two needlework cushions said to have been worked by her own hands and a letter giving instructions to prepare for one of the visits—straw must be scattered in the drive to avoid jolting her carriage, all the ladies of the household must be sent away, and the house must be cleaner than on the last occasion!

This fastidiousness is best enshrined in the story that her passion for personal cleanliness was so great that she had a bath once a month 'whether she needed it or no'. Significantly one of the most famous Elizabethan legends concerns a similar point: if Sir Walter Raleigh did lay down his cloak for the queen to walk upon, then he did it at 'a plashy place' in **Greenwich Park.**

Pedants also believe that there is no foundation for the Essex Ring legend, the story that she gave a ring to the Earl of Essex with an order to return it to her if his life was in danger. He did so, the Countess of Nottingham intercepted it, and he was executed by the queen's warrant, now in the **British Museum.** 'God may forgive you', she told the countess on learning what had happened, 'but I never can'. The ring was inset with the queen's cameo portrait and may be seen in **Westminster Abbey Museum.** For many years it was displayed on her tomb in **Westminster Abbey.**

Refusing to believe that she was dying or even needed to go to bed, she fought for her life on cushions, expiring on the floor at **Richmond Palace** of which hardly a stone remains. She is buried in a restrained tomb of black and white marble designed by Maximilian Colt. Under a high canopy, her bier is supported by lions and her effigy shows her as an old woman, so unlike the portraits which stylised her face in young middle age. Queen Mary, her sister, lies in the same vault and a Latin inscription runs 'Consorts alike of throne and grave, here sleep two sisters, Elizabeth and Mary, in hope of resurrection.'

THE STUARTS

James I (1603-1625)

Born in 1566; great-great-grandson of Henry VII and Elizabeth's nearest relation; succeeded 1603; died 1625.

'The wisest fool in Christendom' and a scholar of sorts, James was a small awkward ungainly man. His hands felt like black satin because he never washed them, his tongue was too large for his mouth, and he was inclined to slobber when kissing his handsome young men. However, since his parents were Mary Queen of Scots and Henry Stewart, Lord Darnley, and he succeeded to the Scottish throne as James VI when only a few months old, he was hardly born with great advantages. He was born in **Edinburgh Castle.**

His succession to the English throne brought the union of the English and Scottish crowns but it is difficult to take James seriously. Surrounded by a posse of favourites, he flits about the Jacobean period, claiming the Divine Right to rule, investigating witches and tobacco, writing polemics, getting drunk. He originated the sport of ' running horses ' in races on Banstead Downs which included **Epsom.** In general he was hopelessly overshadowed by his great predecessor and his doomed son. Even his resting place in **Westminster Abbey** was lost for decades and nothing remains that makes him a noble memory.

The Queen's House, **Greenwich,** was begun for his wife, Anne of Denmark, but quickly abandoned on her death. During his three-day visit in 1617 to **Hoghton Tower** near Preston in Lancashire, he is said to have knighted a loin of excellent beef into a sirloin. One is even shown the long table in the King's Hall on which the joint rested, all very circumstantial for a funny story which is also fathered on Henry VIII and Charles II and is due to mistaken explanations of the French *sur-longe,* above the loin. James stayed twice at **Loseley Park** in Surrey and his bedroom retains its carpet of formidable design—the Tudor Rose, the Crown and the Thistle. Two royal portraits also hang there, commemorating his visit.

Splendid allegorical paintings by Rubens decorate the ceiling of Inigo Jones's **Banqueting House, Whitehall** where James used to attend court masques whose extravagance was matched only by their salacity. They include ' The Union of England and Scotland ', ' The Apotheosis of James I ', and a painting of 400 square feet depicting ' The Benefits of the Government of James I '!

Henry, Prince of Wales

Born in 1594; elder son of James I; died in 1612.

Charles I seems so inevitably the successor of James I that his elder brother Henry, Prince of Wales, is usually overlooked. Henry was born in **Stirling Castle,** one of the greatest monuments in Scotland, its Chapel Royal specially built for his christening. In the **British Museum** is the *Basilikon Doron* which James I composed in his own handwriting for Henry's instruction as an ideal prince. It is now believed that Isaac Oliver's equestrian portrait at **Parham House,** Sussex, always described as of Henry, is of Charles.

At the head of the Grand Staircase in **Windsor Castle** is a suit of armour made for Henry as a boy in about 1610 by the armourers of Greenwich. A gauntlet is missing and may be found in the **Wallace Collection** in London.

Charlton House in south-east London has been described as one of the finest houses of the Jacobean period. It was built between 1607 and 1612 by Adam Newton, Dean of Durham and tutor to Prince Henry. It is now a community centre but the red brick and white stone facings produce the kind of facade that deserves to appear in picture books —but this one rarely does.

The building most often associated with the prince is undoubtedly Inner Temple Gateway, **No. 17 Fleet Street**, described by Pevsner as ' one of the best pieces of half-timber work in London '. It was built in about 1610-11, contains its original plaster ceiling and carved oak panels, and has always been identified as the Council Chamber of the Duchy of Cornwall when Prince Henry was Duke of Cornwall. A less respectful theory suggests that the ' P.H. ' in the plaster may refer to the ' Prince's Arms ', a tavern which stood in the area in about 1612.

The prince died of typhoid and is buried in Mary Queen of Scots' vault in **Westminster Abbey**, together with many other loose ends of the Stuart dynasty—including Elizabeth of Bohemia, the 'Winter Queen ', Prince Rupert, and Queen Anne's children.

Charles I (1625-1649)

Born in 1600; surviving son of James I; succeeded in 1625; executed in 1649.

It was to Sir Walter Raleigh that his judges said ' You have lived like a star, at which the world hath gazed; and like a star you must fall, when the firmament is shaked ', but these words apply equally to Charles I. The exquisite pleasures of his early life were ended by Civil War and execution. It is so easy to see Charles I's England as peopled by characters out of Van Dyck portraits that most moderns are Cavaliers from childhood. Only experience shows us that there was another type of life and that its supporters were not demons incarnate.

In his happier days Charles was a splendid patron of the arts, commissioning Van Dyck to paint his court and Rubens to decorate the ceiling of his **Banqueting House** in

Whitehall. Apart from the superb portraits, few things show us the Charles of this earlier time. His cradle is in the Long Gallery at **Hatfield House.** His ebony and mother-of-pearl inlaid walking stick is at **Woburn Abbey.** The most tangible relic of the early years is the Queen's House, **Greenwich,** begun in 1617 for Charles's mother, Anne of Denmark, but completed in 1635 for his wife, Henrietta Maria. It was a landmark in architecture, the first building designed in Britain in strictly classical Palladian style. Its furnishings and gardens have disappeared, and Charles's gorgeous pictures have been replaced by those of the National Maritime Museum, but we can never forget that it was known in the 1630s as the ' House of Delight'.

In the simplest terms, Charles wanted absolute power, ruled without Parliament for eleven years and raised money illegally. This finally caused a Parliamentary struggle leading to civil war. The first battle of the war was fought in the king's presence at **Edgehill,** Warwickshire, on 23rd October 1642, but was indecisive. The precipice and field of battle remain well preserved and by coincidence are War Department property.

One takes one's choice of the later battles—**Chalgrove Field, Newbury** and others were mere skirmishes with ordinary life at first continuing in their midst. Peace still seemed possible and early in 1645 Charles and Cromwell met with their commissioners in the Old Treaty House, now the Crown Inn, at **Uxbridge,** Greater London. Their negotiations lasted twenty days and were unsuccessful. The royal cause was lost when Charles was defeated at **Naseby** in Northamptonshire on 14th June 1645, but the war continued for some time. Charles is said to have watched his army's defeat at **Rowton Heath** shortly afterwards from King Charles's Tower, **Chester,** which now contains a Civil War exhibition (plate 18). At **Newark** he surrendered to the Scottish army which handed him over to the English Parliament. They took him to Holdenby or **Holmby Hall,** a few miles south of Naseby and, although the house was rebuilt last century, a holly avenue is still called the King's Walk. Since Parliament wished to disband the Army and come to terms with Charles, an army officer, Cornet Joyce, removed the king from Holmby after four months there and placed him in the custody of the Army. Charles escaped to the Isle of Wight but his continual intrigues with potential supporters led first to his imprisonment in **Carisbrooke Castle** from 1647 and ultimately to the idea of trial and execution. Both his attempts to escape from Carisbrooke were unsuccessful. The castle is now the Isle of Wight Museum. It contains several relics of the king, his signed Book of Common Prayer, the key of his prison room and the handle of his walking stick.

He was brought to **Westminster Hall,** Britain's chief law-court from 1224 to 1882, and tried for the high treason of making war against his subjects. A tablet marks the spot where he sat and where he was condemned to death. His chair may be the one shown in the Victoria and Albert Museum, and his death warrant is in the House of Lords Library. Charles was executed at his own front door, on a scaffold in the street outside the **Banqueting House, Whitehall,** all that was then built and all that now remains of the foremost Stuart palace, destroyed by fire in 1698.

Execution made the king seem a martyr, so the preservation of relics and memories gives us a remarkably complete picture of him on that last day, 30th January 1649. The blue knitted silk vest he wore on the scaffold is in the **Museum of London,** with the gloves and fragments of the cloak. The shirt is owned by the Queen. The doublet is at **Longleat;** it was there as early as Charles II's reign and lacks many of its buttons which were given away as mementoes of the dead king. Pieces of his neckcloth and of his cloak lining, with the ivory knob from another walking stick, are in Christchurch Mansion, **Ipswich.** Part of his lace cravat and the nightcap he wore on the night before his execution are in **Carisbrooke Castle.**

Among those present at the execution was the seventeen-year-old Philip Henry who noted in his diary: ' The blow I saw given and can truly say with a sad heart, at the instant whereof, I remember well, there was such a groan by the thousands then present as I never heard before and desire I may never hear again '.

Charles is buried in Henry VIII's vault in St. George's Chapel, **Windsor.** As his coffin was borne through Windsor Castle, snow fell until the black velvet pall was covered in white—the colour of innocence.

At **Charing Cross** on the site of Edward I's Eleanor cross (see page 15) stands the bronze statue of Charles I, made in 1633 by Le Sueur (plate 15). Even nowadays Royalist sympathisers place wreaths by the statue on the anniversary of his execution.

THE INTERREGNUM (1649-1660)

Here ruled :
    The Rump of the Long Parliament (1649-1653)
    Oliver Cromwell, Lord Protector (1653-1658)
    Richard Cromwell, his son (1658-1659)
    There was then a Parliamentary interregnum until the restoration of the monarchy in 1660.

Charles II (1660-1685)

Born in 1630; eldest son of Charles I; king at the restoration of the monarchy in 1660 (or, strictly speaking, from 1649); died in 1685.

Charles II was born at **St. James's Palace.** He is among the strongest contenders for the title of everyone's favourite king. Tall, dark, extremely handsome, cynically good-natured, a wit and a devil with the women, his flippancy was a facade to his very great intelligence. The narrow-minded will dismiss him as simply a rake or a profligate, but how can one fail to warm to a man reported to have taken communion with three bishops on one side and three bastard sons by three different mistresses on the other?

On 1st January 1651 when he was twenty years old, he was crowned king by the Scots at **Scone.** He marched into England, was proclaimed king at Worcester in August, and was then stopped and defeated at the battle of **Worcester** on Cromwell's lucky day, 3rd September. Charles watched most of the battle from the cathedral tower though he led a charge and was almost captured in a house in Corn Market. A remnant of this house, once a half-timbered mansion dated 1577 but largely destroyed by fire in 1799, is marked by a tablet on its wall showing a crown in an oak tree. This alludes to the days after Charles's escape from Worcester when he came to **Boscobel House** in Salop, a small seventeenth-century manor-house then surrounded by dense woods (plate 20). Part of his time there he spent in an oak tree near the house, though the present 'Royal Oak' is probably only a descendant of the original which not even a high fence could preserve from souvenir hunters. A monument to 'Unparallel'd Pendrell, preserver and conductor to his Majesty' at this time is in **St. Giles-in-the-Fields church,** London, and pensions are still paid to his family. Charles is also said to have sheltered in **Moseley Old Hall** near Wolverhampton, where his bed and hiding place may be seen. On 23rd September 1651 Charles stayed at the Old George Inn, **Bridport,** Dorset, now a chemist's shop (plate 19). The town was full of Parliamentary troops, and despite his disguise as a groom he only narrowly avoided recognition by an ostler in the inn-yard. He escaped to **Trent** Manor near Sherborne, where he stayed twelve days before finally escaping to France from **Shoreham,** Sussex, in the coal-brig *Surprise* (renamed *The Royal Escape* on his Restoration), whose captain, Nicholas Tettersell, is buried in the churchyard of St. Nicholas, **Brighton.**

In 1660 he was recalled to England. On 28th May 1660, the night before his thirtieth birthday and his state entry into London, Charles stayed at the red-brick Elizabethan mansion now called Restoration House, **Rochester.** The following day has ever since been commemorated as Oak Apple Day. One of the ceremonies is held at **Chelsea Hospital,** the old soldiers' home which he founded, where his statue is decorated with oak leaves. Charles was welcomed to London by both Houses of Parliament, an event he must have viewed with mixed feelings since it was staged in the **Banqueting House, Whitehall,** the very room from which his father had walked to the scaffold eleven years before.

After the restoration of the monarchy, Charles is little connected with individual places. Determined, in his own euphemistic phrase, never to go on his travels again, he began earning his history-book title, the Merry Monarch. His foundation of the Royal Society and his wars with France are ignored in the popular imagination. We see him as a keen patron of the turf and the theatre, strolling in **St. James's Park** with a mistress on each arm, swapping vulgar repartee with Nell Gwyn, flashing the irresistible charm which is still so often apparent. The collection of treasures in the **Oxford Divinity School** includes a sheet of notes passed back and forth between the king and Lord Clarendon at some doubtless fearfully dull meeting. Each adds a line at a time, Clarendon's remarks becoming increasingly agitated because the king insists on visiting his sister at **Tunbridge Wells** with only his night bag. Clarendon is almost apoplectic: ' God, you will not go without 40 or 50 horse!' Back comes the answer smoothly: ' I count that part of my night bag'.

Charles is buried in **Westminster Abbey** and our last view of him is in **Westminster Abbey Museum.** Staring over our heads, his funeral effigy of 1685 wears the oppressive lace, velvet, cloth of silver and ruffles of the period, cloaked and hatted in the oldest Garter robes in Britain. This is the earliest complete funeral effigy in the Abbey's collection and is almost certainly based on a death mask, which prompted someone in 1695 to write: ''tis to ye life and truly to admiration'. The naughty Lord Rochester summed up Charles's character succinctly if unfairly:

> Here lies our sovereign lord the King
> Whose promise none relies on;
> He never said a foolish thing,
> Nor ever did a wise one.

Nell Gwyn
Born in 1650; died in 1687.

Nell Gwyn has become one of the folk heroines of the British public, but there are few relics of her—a marble bust ascribed to Grinling Gibbons, the letters 'E G' boldly scrawled in her account at **Child's Bank** in London, her burial in the vicar's vault of Old **St. Martin's-in-the-Fields** in 1687—but Nell's fame lives mostly in stories. They were handed down by her commoner contemporaries, people who shared her background, who saw her as warm-hearted and good-natured. Even courtiers knew that she was faithful and honest. She did nothing to provoke jealousy. She had no illusions about what she was: born in **Hereford** or perhaps in London, brought up in a brothel in **Drury Lane,** an orange-seller at the Theatre Royal who had become an actress, then been lucky enough to attract the king's eye. That was what made her ' pretty, witty Nell' and brought her to the mind of the dying Charles II. If his last words to his brother James were not ' Let not poor Nelly starve', as everyone believes, then they should have been.

One appreciates the best story about her quick impudence by recalling that the king's other mistresses, the Duchesses of Cleveland, Portsmouth and Mazarin, were all Roman Catholics. One day Nell's carriage was stoned by a crowd who thought it contained the hated ' Madam Carwell', Louise de Kéroualle, Duchess of Portsmouth. Without hesitation, Nell stuck her head out of the window shouting 'Don't hurt me, good people! I'm the Protestant whore!' She was cheered home.

James II (1685-1688)
Born in 1633; second son of Charles I; succeeded his brother Charles II in 1685; deposed in 1688; died in exile in 1701.

His whole character can be summarised in one

anecdote. He rebuked Charles II for walking in the park without a guard, to which Charles replied 'I am sure no man in England will take away my life to make you King.'

James was born in **St. James's Palace.** As a young man he had shown himself to be a naval commander of considerable ability and courage. He is linked with his naval contemporary, Samuel Pepys the diarist, by an ivory chess-set, a gift from the king, now in the **Museum of London.** Despite this popular talent, James's stern and uncompromising Roman Catholicism seemed bound to cause trouble.

As king he sought despotic power, for which one instance will suffice. In 1687 he failed to compel the fellows of Magdalen College, **Oxford,** to elect his unworthy nominee as their president, even going to Oxford himself to press the point. When his second unqualified candidate was also rejected, he expelled both fellows and undergraduates, showing that no loyalty nor legal condition could prevail against his royal caprice. James regained no popularity when he yielded and the 144-foot high Perpendicular tower of Magdalen, perhaps the finest in Britain and certainly the most famous view in Oxford, has ever since been called the tower against which James II ran his head.

He had followed an indiscreetly zealous pro-Catholic policy since the Duke of Monmouth was defeated. Monmouth was Charles II's eldest and favourite son, unfortunately illegitimate but Protestant and popular. He invaded England in 1685, only to have his peasant army routed among the Somerset marshes at **Sedgemoor** near Taunton. Matters came to head with the birth of James's son in 1688 for it was rumoured that the baby had arrived so conveniently on time to establish a Roman Catholic dynasty that it had been put into the queen's bed in a warming-pan. Men now turned to James's Protestant daughter Mary and her Dutch husband William of Orange, inviting them to become joint sovereigns of Britain.

James placed a wrought-iron weathercock on the north end of the **Banqueting House** roof in Whitehall, watching it from his window to see when William might sail. A week later the wind began blowing from the north, the 'Protestant Wind' which allowed William to sail for **Torbay** and **Brixham** where he landed (plate 21). James's queen, Mary of Modena, and their baby escaped to France through **Gravesend,** with James following shortly after, despite a false start which involved his being captured by fishermen. They held him captive for a time in 12 Market Place, **Faversham,** which

was then an inn, but at last he got free—perhaps he was
allowed to escape to save embarrassment all round. It says
much for James's touching faith in the rule of law that before
he escaped he thought he had stopped the revolution—by
throwing the Great Seal of England into the Thames!

The Jacobites

In 1688 a son was born to James II at **St. James's Palace.**
Furious Protestants said that the baby was supposititious,
introduced into the queen's bed in a warming-pan to ensure
the Roman Catholic succession to the British throne. The
four-poster bed with its original heavily embroidered hangings
is at **Kensington Palace.** The child was legitimate but any
putative warming-pan has been lost.

The Glorious Revolution of 1688 deposed James II who
held an increasingly pious court in exile at Saint Germain,
where a memorial records his death in 1701. The Act of
Settlement of that year allowed only Protestants to succeed to
the British throne, the measure that finally brought us
George I. James II's son, James Edward Stuart, was known
as the Old Pretender—the elder claimant to the throne—
and his supporters as Jacobites, from Jacobus, the Latin for
James. In 1701 he was proclaimed King James III by
Louis XIV of France and in 1715 he invaded Scotland, his
family's original kingdom. A Highland rising in his favour
was checked at **Sheriffmuir** and, after landing briefly at
Peterhead, James retreated home to France. He died in Rome
in 1766 after a legitimist reign of over sixty-four years and
is buried in St. Peter's with his two sons.

The elder, Charles Edward Stuart (1720-1788), the Young
Pretender, the Young Chevalier, Bonnie Prince Charlie, was a
figure of misapplied Scots romance who was quarter Anglo-
Polish, quarter Italian, quarter French, and quarter German.
Charles's rising of 1745 began well with a victory over George
II's troops at **Prestonpans.** He held court in the Palace of
Holyroodhouse in **Edinburgh,** while personal relics and
memories are scattered throughout the city. Some of his
clothes are displayed in Edinburgh Castle. **Carlisle** surrendered
without a fight and he proclaimed his father as James III
in the market-place, then set up headquarters at Highmoor
House, 42 English Street, a site now marked by plaques.
The chair in which he slept and other possessions are in the
city museum. He marched through **Penrith,** where there are
minor Jacobite associations, and on as far south as **Derby**
where the museum has oak panelling from the room in which

he held his last council of war. His ceremonial shield inlaid with silver is at **Warwick Castle.** From Derby he retreated to Scotland where his rising failed utterly with the rout at **Culloden** in 1746, the Jacobites' final appearance as a serious political force.

Sentimental Jacobitism continued to flourish. William III had died after his horse had stumbled on a molehill, so toasts were made to 'the little gentleman in black velvet' and, until the accession of Edward VII in 1901, finger bowls were never placed on British royal dinner tables because secret sympathisers once drank to 'the king over the water'. Drinking glasses were engraved with Stuart portraits, a rose with one or two buds, and other mysterious allusions. There is a fine collection of these glasses in the **Museum of London** and a smaller one in the **Birmingham Museum,** while there is also a large Jacobite section in the West Highland Museum at **Fort William,** Inverness-shire. The legitimists' Charles III died in 1788 and his brother Henry (1725-1807) was regarded as Henry IX. This last prince of the House of Stuart had become a cardinal in 1747 and sentiment was already so entrenched that he was granted a pension by the British crown.

The Stuart claim reverted at his death to the descendants of Charles II's favourite sister Minette, or Henrietta Duchess of Orleans. Sentimental Jacobitism mostly collapsed about 1914 when the 'rightful' sovereign of England was found to be the Queen of Bavaria. Today her grandson, Albrecht, has the claim or, if he is barred by an earlier uncle-niece marriage, the present Stuart pretender to the British throne is the Duke of Parma.

John Byrom, the eighteenth-century Jacobite versifier, saw the problem clearly:

> God bless the King, I mean the Faith's Defender;
> God bless—no harm in blessing—the Pretender;
> But who Pretender is, or who is King,
> God bless us all—that's quite another thing.

William III (1689-1702) and Mary II (1689-1694)

Mary: born in 1662; elder daughter of James II. William: born in 1650; grandson of Charles I. William and Mary joint sovereigns of Britain in 1689. Mary died in 1694; William in 1702.

Mary, James II's elder daughter by his Protestant first wife Anne Hyde, was born at **St. James's Palace,** and married

William of Orange, who was born at The Hague in 1650. They make a fascinating couple, this king and queen by invitation. William was an aloof, taciturn, unpopular Dutchman. Mary was a lively, talkative, ordinary woman who could never remember who she was or where she was. The first thing she did on entering a new palace was to run round feeling all the beds and chattering about cupboard space, which shocked the servants immoderately.

William landed at **Brixham** quay—the very stone is marked —on 5th November 1688 (plate 21) and issued his Proclamation to the English people at **Sherborne.** He and Mary were invited to become joint sovereigns with the survivor to reign alone, and the crown was offered to them in the **Banqueting House, Whitehall.** Their joint coronation required a substitute Coronation Chair for Mary, which now stands in **Westminster Abbey Museum.**

William suffered from asthma and learned that the air in the then country village of **Kensington** would give relief. He would also be free from ceremonial but near Westminster, so in 1689 he bought Nottingham House which Wren reconstructed after the manner of Versailles and called **Kensington Palace.** This was the British monarch's chief residence from 1689 to 1760 and, although decorated later in grander style by William Kent for George I, the State Apartments include several suites from the original scheme, with superb oak panelling, carving and ironwork.

Attention turned next to **Hampton Court** where much of the picturesque but inconvenient Tudor palace was demolished by Wren who rebuilt it in a series of rooms which are the acme of late seventeenth-century elegance and comfort. Mary started the domestic hobby of collecting ornamental china and the tiered chimney pieces at Hampton Court were constructed especially to display her collection. William's writing table is also there.

As a thank-offering for the naval victory of La Hogue, Mary decided to found a hospital for old or disabled seamen on the lines of the soldiers' hospital at Chelsea. She died of smallpox in 1694 but William encouraged the project as her memorial. Greenwich Hospital is now known as the **Royal Naval College, Greenwich,** but retains what may be the finest range of buildings in this country. Begun in 1696 in the English Baroque style, their construction lasted half a century under the direction of Wren, Vanbrugh and Hawksmoor. The masterpiece is the Painted Hall, originally the pensioners' dining hall, completed in 1704 but covered by a ceiling which took Sir James Thornhill twenty years to paint, being completed in 1727. This ceiling, 106 feet long by 51 feet 6 inches broad, is one of Britain's greatest treasures. It shows William and Mary attended by Peace, Concord and the Four Virtues. The king's feet are on Tyranny as he offers the cap of liberty to Europe. The central group is surrounded by a swarm of figures and trophies, while the Upper Hall shows William's landing at Torbay and the Return of the Golden Age under George I. Not forgotten, Queen Anne is painted on the Upper Hall ceiling. For painting the *trompe l'oeil* walls Thornhill received £1 a square yard with £3 a square yard for the ceiling.

In 1702 the king was riding in the park at **Hampton Court** when his favourite horse Sorrel stumbled and threw him. A trivial accident caused a possible broken collar-bone but the king was brought back to **Kensington Palace** where he died in King William's Gallery.

When William and Mary died, effigies were made to stand by their graves in **Westminster Abbey** as a tourist attraction. They stand today in **Westminster Abbey Museum,** looking as if they are in the middle of an interrupted conversation. Mary is tall, plump and wears a large double chin. William is memorable for two things: even on a special plinth he is noticeably shorter than his wife, and one sees why his vast nose reminded contemporaries of an eagle's beak.

Anne (1702-1714)

Born in 1665; second daughter of James II by Anne Hyde; succeeded her brother-in-law William III in 1702; died in 1714.

Arguably the dullest person ever to sit on the English throne, Anne would have enjoyed the life of the more vegetable kind of housewife. Born in **St. James's Palace,** completely ordinary and married to a foreign nonentity, she found friendship with the brilliant Sarah Jennings, later Duchess of Marlborough—and made it into homely chit-chat between herself as 'Mrs Morley' and the Duchess as 'Mrs Freeman'.

Against this dowdiness we must set the heroic way in which she endured the drudgery of routine official duties and the continual great pain she suffered from dropsy, gout and over-eating. She had at least fifteen children who all died young. In her final years she was a pathetic figure, amazingly fat, swathed in bandages, having to be carried upstairs in a chair. Finally, it is said, she had to be lowered through trapdoors. The magnificent age of Queen Anne is nothing to do with her.

She was extremely fond of **Kensington Palace** where she directed the laying out of the gardens and where the Orangery was built for her in 1705, a fine airy building of orange brick perhaps designed by Wren. In August 1711 she moved the main Windsor races, another of her pastimes, from Datchet to **Ascot** and so founded the famous meeting. She died at **Kensington Palace** and is buried in Henry VII's Chapel, **Westminster Abbey.**

There are very few places where one can feel close to Queen Anne. **Blenheim Palace,** Oxfordshire, was the nation's gift to her greatest general John Churchill, first Duke of Marlborough, and the husband of her great friend, Sarah Jennings, for his victories over Louis XIV. It is Vanbrugh's master-piece, built between 1705 and 1722 in baroque style, one of Britain's largest and greatest houses. Its gardens are by Capability Brown, its ceilings by Laguerre and Thornhill, its carving by Grinling Gibbons. The nominal rent is a banner bearing the ancient arms of France, three gold lilies on a white ground. This is paid annually on 13th August, the anniversary of Blenheim, and kept in the Guard Chamber at **Windsor Castle.**

Where Queen Anne is concerned the grotesque and pathetic are continually tripped up by the incongruous. She was popularly believed to console herself with 'cold tea'—brandy from a tea-cup. Her wax effigy in **Westminster Abbey Museum** wore a supremely unbecoming black wig, from 1768 to 1971, and still wears an unflattering dress and a crown which is too small. She may be summed up in two proverbial phrases: 'Good Queen Anne' and 'Queen Anne is dead'. There is a third: 'God save Queen Log'.

THE HANOVERIANS

George I (1714-1727)

Born in 1660; son of James I's daughter's daughter; succeeded in 1714; died in 1727.

George I was a despotic German elector, stolid and unimaginative, who spoke no English but whose descent from James I made him Queen Anne's nearest Protestant heir.

He was born in Hanover, lived in Hanover, died in Hanover and was buried in Hanover. He would willingly have yielded a square mile of England to add a square yard to Hanover and we felt the same way about him.

George II (1727-1760)

Born in 1683; only son of George I; succeeded in 1727; died in 1760.

George II was still essentially a German—he was born in Hanover—but at least a more attractive one. He was a soldier, the last English king to lead his troops into battle—at his victory of Dettingen in 1743—and his reign saw the conquest of Canada and India. He was above all things methodical and regular so that a contemporary said ' He seems to think his having done a thing today an unanswerable reason for his doing it tomorrow'.

As Prince of Wales he seems to have lived in the early eighteenth-century red-brick house called Marlow Place at **Marlow** in Buckinghamshire. When he became king, rooms at **Hampton Court** were fitted up for himself and his queen, Caroline. We learn that the queen's chaplain used to read morning prayers in the Queen's Private Chapel, while she dressed in the Queen's Bathing Closet or Dressing Room next door with the door ajar! In one wall is a marble-lined recess with a basin and, royal luxury, a tap for cold running water. The bed in which George II died at **Kensington Palace** became a perquisite of his Lord Chamberlain, the fourth Duke of Devonshire, and is now in the State Bedroom at **Chatsworth.** The king had been deeply shocked by his wife's death and at his burial, the last of a king of England in **Westminster Abbey,** the two coffins were placed together and their sides removed so that the remains could mingle in death. It was a macabre yet loving gesture.

Frederick Lewis, Prince of Wales

Born in 1707; elder son of George II; died in 1751, before his father.

His portrait is in the State Dining Room at **Warwick Castle,** painted in 1738 and less interesting for the sitter than for the splendidly ornate carved and gilded frame surrounding the prince with military trophies and drums. A companion portrait of his wife Augusta and their son, the future George III, hangs beside it. The frame is equally ornate, this time with a statue of Fame blowing a trumpet. The prince's scarlet and gold barge of 1732 is in the Barge House at the National Maritime Museum, **Greenwich.** He was born in Hanover, and is buried in **Westminster Abbey.**

' Poor Fred ' was an indistinct figure, notable only for his shattering mediocrity :

> Here lies Fred,
> Who was alive and is dead :
> Had it been his father
> I had much rather
> But since 'tis only Fred,
> Who was alive and is dead—
> There's no more to be said.

George III (1760-1820)

Born in 1738; eldest son of Frederick Lewis, Prince of Wales; succeeded his grandfather George II in 1760; died in 1820.

' Born and educated in this country, I glory in the name of Britain'. The young George III wrote out these words for inclusion in his first Speech from the Throne and they are displayed on their original slip of paper in the **British Museum.** He was indeed born here, in London, at **Norfolk House, St. James's,** since demolished. A king whose reign spanned sixty years, who had both Pitts as prime ministers, and was partly responsible for losing the American colonies is obviously an interesting political figure, but George III is easily approachable on a more intimate scale. His exemplary domestic life and simple pleasures—he was nicknamed ' Farmer George '—made him seem more of a local squire than a king and he was enormously popular in middle life. For all his turkey-cock look and staccato ' What ! ? What ! ? ' he was one of our most endearing monarchs.

Among his first actions as king in 1762 was to buy Buckingham House, later completely remodelled by Nash. As recently as 1913 the front was rebuilt in Portland stone from designs by Webb to make it one of the best-known London sights, **Buckingham Palace.** George's growing children, fifteen in all, spent their time in houses at Kew, and the whole family passed many secluded summers at the jolly little seventeenth-century red-brick Dutch House in Kew Gardens which masquerades under the title **Kew Palace** (plate 22). This was their favourite residence and contains a collection of personal trivia—their toys, their smelling bottles and snuff-boxes. Nearby is **Queen's Cottage,** built about 1772 as a summerhouse where princesses could give tea-parties. It is in *cottage orné* style, artificially rural but with every necessary comfort, even if the roof is thatched and one room made to look like a tent.

Between 1789 and 1805, the royal family enjoyed summer holidays at the seaside, at **Weymouth,** the English Naples. They stayed at Gloucester Lodge, now the Gloucester Hotel, and the king actually bathed in the sea with a full band round him to play an anthem as he emerged from his bathing machine. The atmosphere during one of his holidays is described in Thomas Hardy's *The Trumpet Major*. On the Esplanade at Weymouth is 'The King's Statue', a brightly painted statue of George erected in 1809 to commemorate his jubilee and 'as a memorial to future ages of the virtues of the monarch'. Two miles east of Weymouth is the **White Horse,** a chalk figure cut out of the downland turf in 1808 and representing George III on horseback. Tactlessly the figure trots away from the town.

The mahogany writing-table that the king used for forty years is in the Museum of London collection. It still bears the blotter, quill pen, inkstand and ruler that were there on the last day he used it, but George was also a practical man. He once argued about the production of beef and asked why people did not plant more. Unconvinced by the answer that beef was not grown like a vegetable, he planted some pieces in his garden at Kew, or so it was said.

George III is inextricably linked with **Windsor Castle.** In earlier happier days he delighted to walk with his family on the terraces there, bowing to the public who had been admitted and questioning the Eton schoolboys on their studies. It was in **Windsor Great Park** that he shook hands with an oak tree, conversing with it under the mistaken impression that it was the King of Prussia. The king showed signs of temporary madness as early as 1788 and 1804 but late in 1810 he became finally and totally deranged. It seems to have been proved that he was not suffering from mental insanity but from porphyria, a physical disease with similar results. His eldest son was appointed Prince Regent and the pitiful old king was moved from Queen's Lodge to the private apartments of Windsor Castle. There he dragged out his last decade under restraint, a pathetic white-bearded figure, supposedly mad in an age unsympathetic to such a condition, nearly blind, shambling through his rooms in a flannel dressing-gown and ermine nightcap.

He is buried at **Windsor,** in a vault under St. George's Chapel. Neither his last years nor his tombful of mutually antipathetic relations are pleasant matters on which to end. Our last view of him should be his equestrian statue by Westmacott, erected in 1831 on Snow Hill at the far end of the Long Walk in **Windsor Great Park.** It is called the Copper Horse. It gives him a good view of the castle whose rooms he always found uninhabitable and the country whose shores he never left throughout his eighty-two years.

George IV (1820-1830)
Born in 1762; eldest son of George III; Prince Regent from 1810; succeeded as king in 1820; died in 1830.

> By his bulk and by his size,
> By his oily qualities,
> This (or else my eyesight fails),
> This should be the Prince of Whales.

In *The Triumph of the Whale,* Charles Lamb described only one face of a Janus character. It is our pleasure to see both. For all that he was the eldest of that crowd of villainously slapstick comedians, the sons of George III, the young Prince of Wales was undeniably attractive. Handsome, clever, and endowed with superb aesthetic taste, he left the homely seclusion of **St. James's Palace,** where he was born, and **Kew Palace,** where his high chair and fishing rod may still be seen, for a life of fashion.

From 1783 his main official residence was Carlton House on the north side of **The Mall** where the Duke of York's Column stands. Its portico now graces the **National Gallery** in Trafalgar Square for the house was demolished in 1826. Also in 1783, on 7th September, he paid his first visit to the Sussex village of Brighthelmstone, where medicinal sea-bathing was in vogue. From that day on, he visited what is now **Brighton** constantly for forty-four years.

Two years later he secretly and morganatically married

Mrs. Maria Fitzherbert, a marriage which for an ordinary man would have been perfectly legal. Unfortunately Mrs. Fitzherbert was a Roman Catholic and the 1701 Act of Settlement stated that a royal heir who married a Roman Catholic forfeited his right to the throne. Moreover, since the Royal Marriage Act of 1772, the king's consent was needed for a royal marriage and it had not been sought. They lived quietly by the sea at **Brighton** and in 1786 George leased a house in the Steine. The following year Henry Holland rebuilt it as a small but elegant seaside villa where the Prince lived each summer and Christmas for several years. Mrs. Fitzherbert lived in a house in the Steine, and never spent a night at the Royal Pavilion.

The prince's selfishness, extravagance and dissipation must have been growing for the next twenty years but the other Janus face appeared when his father seemed totally insane and George became Regent in 1810.

Between 1815 and 1822 his surveyor-general John Nash had rebuilt the villa at **Brighton** to form the Brighton Pavilion. Onion domes sprouted from it, pinnacles, minarets. It was—and is—Indian outside and Chinese inside. Scarlet and gold blare against yellow, pink and blue. There is a ceiling like a palm tree and a dragon snakes above one's head, holding a chandelier in its claws. Rosewood pianos are inlaid with brass. Individual splendours and overblown magnificence produce the fantasticated beauty of a fairy tale palace or a choice essay on the appallingly vulgar, depending on one's point of view. A remark popularly attributed to Sydney Smith, suggesting that St. Paul's Cathedral must have pupped, is a syncopated version of a comment by William Wilberforce. He admired the Pavilion as being ' beautiful and tasty . . . though it looks very much as if St. Paul's had come down to the sea and left behind a litter of cupolas'.

In the middle of this hothouse was the rapidly fattening Prinny, the ludicrous master of an exotic court, practically the British Grand Sophy. His enormous debts and reckless extravagance brought him extreme unpopularity. His sense of responsibility was non-existent.

Only once can we feel much sympathy for him. His wife Caroline was as ridiculous and grotesque as he was, but they had an only child, Charlotte. In 1817 George was staying with the Marquess of Hertford—his bed, complete with carved ostrich feathers, is shown at **Ragley Hall** in Warwickshire—when news came that the princess was seriously ill. Within a few days she had died in childbirth at her home,

Claremont near Esher in Surrey, and the course of history was altered towards Queen Victoria. Charlotte is buried in St. George's Chapel, **Windsor,** where her memorial in white marble shows her rising from the tomb between angels, making one think of muslin and dimity and women like Jane Austen. Alas, it seems that Charlotte was very much the child of her parents, a blowzy, noisy Hanoverian hoyden.

As ' The First Gentleman of Europe ', he had entertained the Allied sovereigns in the garden at **Carlton House** in 1814, receiving them in a canvas pavilion nearly forty yards across which was moved to **Woolwich** in 1819 and encased in metal. Known as the Rotunda, it houses a museum of artillery and the canvas survived until its removal in 1974. Nash designed the Rotunda as he designed the **Regents Park Terraces.** These wonderful houses surround Regents Park and were linked by Nash's earlier Regent Street to Carlton House, a splendid piece of town planning which must be at least partly attributed to the Regent's patronage of the arts.

Inevitably he became king. His coronation robes are in the State Apartments at **Windsor Castle** but by now he was at the stage of pink tights, spit curls and greasepaint, as well as oglingly sentimental relationships with old women. He did much harm to the monarchy and sank into an unmourned grave in St. George's Chapel, **Windsor.**

Mrs. Fitzherbert died in 1837 and her tomb in the then very new Roman Catholic church of St. John the Baptist, **Kemp Town,** Brighton, shows her effigy wearing three wedding rings, for George was her third husband. Like Nell Gwyn, Mrs. Fitzherbert is considered notorious, but in her case the reputation is very largely unjustified.

William IV (1830-1837)

Born in 1765; younger brother of George IV; succeeded in 1830; died in 1837.

Although he was a dutiful supporter of parliamentary and social reform we remember him as a genial, blundering ass of a man, most happy as a young officer in the Navy when, incidentally, he became the only British prince to see British New York. He was also celebrated for spending twenty years as Duke of Clarence in blissful domesticity with Mrs. Jordan the actress, fat, coarse and the love of his life. They lived at **Petersham Lodge** in Richmond Park where they were quietly forgotten, then at Bushy by Hampton

Court where he became Ranger of Bushy Park and was again quietly forgotten. Their home, the early eighteenth-century **Bushy House** (plate 24), is near the Teddington end of the magnificent mile-long chestnut avenue.

As a result of Princess Charlotte's death in 1817 the duke was forced to marry a suitable bride but, despite his crew of ten little Fitzclarences, he failed to produce a male heir. He succeeded to the throne at George IV's death and achieved a matchless reputation as Silly Billy, the Sailor King with a gift for telling blue jokes at improper times, swearing at slipshod sailors, chattering away in **Portsmouth Dockyard** to anyone who would listen, and generally getting under people's feet. Even his statue had to be removed from King William Street in the City because it held up the traffic. It now stands neatly tucked away on a lawn beside King William Walk, **Greenwich.**

He was born in **Buckingham Palace** and is buried in St. George's Chapel, **Windsor.** His queen, Adelaide, died in 1849 at Bentley Priory, **Stanmore,** in north-west London.

Victoria (1837-1901)

Born in 1819; daughter of Edward Duke of Kent, fourth son of George III; succeeded her uncle William IV in 1837; died in 1901.

Victoria's reign of sixty-four years, the longest of any British sovereign, means that the personal memories we have of her from people still living are of a little old lady in black, wearing a small crown over white lace, at a pinnacle of respect and love. She is seen as the mother figure of a century and of an empire. It is all summed up in the words carved in the pavement before the steps of **St. Paul's Cathedral:** ' Here Queen Victoria returned thanks to Almighty God for the sixtieth anniversary of her accession, June 22, 1897 '. Much happened before that.

Although she became the first monarch to live regularly at **Buckingham Palace,** Victoria was born at **Kensington Palace.** She spent her childhood there and dozens of items still evoke her memory: her toys, dolls she dressed when a child, her dolls' house. At 6 a.m. on 20th June 1837 she was called from the bedroom she shared with her mother to be greeted as queen and it was at Kensington Palace later that same morning that she held her first council. Her coronation robes are in the **Museum of London** collection, together with the dress she wore at her wedding in 1840 at the Chapel

Royal, **St. James's.** The swing-cot used for all her children is still at Kensington Palace. Three more of her dresses, including the uniform she wore in 1856 at the first Victoria Cross investiture and her last dress in deep mourning, all proving her tiny stature, are also in the Museum of London collection. Other personal relics, including a nightdress, handkerchief and stockings, are preserved at **Woburn Abbey.**

Reacting against the horror stories told about her wicked uncles, the young queen managed to rehabilitate the British monarchy, helped by her German husband Albert, later Prince Consort, whose excellent qualities were not generally appreciated until after his death. It was Albert who bought **Balmoral Castle** in Aberdeenshire to serve as a holiday residence for his family. He rebuilt it in white granite and the baronial style with tartan everywhere including the carpets. It still remains the present queen's private property but the gardens are open to the public and one can see Queen Victoria's garden cottage there.

After Albert's death in 1861 the queen lived in seclusion for many years, becoming increasingly unpopular before she was encouraged to appear in public again. She was often referred to as the ' Widow of Windsor ', but her favourite home was **Osborne House** in the Isle of Wight. Prince Albert purchased the estate in 1845 and, because the view over the Solent reminded him of the Bay of Naples—it must have changed, he helped Thomas Cubitt to design a house in the Italian style. After 1861 Victoria tried to keep both house and contents completely unaltered as a memorial to her husband. The State Apartments remain unaltered, rooms frozen in a past era. One feels sure that the queen and Prince Albert will come back through the door at any moment. Their writing tables are still side by side, where the prince would draft the queen's letters; family portraits and photographs are everywhere. In the grounds are the queen's bathing machine and her children's garden tools and wheelbarrows. A short walk from the gates is St. Mildred's Church, **Whippingham,** packed with memories of the queen and her family. However, one is irresistibly drawn back to the State Apartments, to the queen's elevator-lift, to her bathroom, to the indoor gates which cut her off from ordinary mortals, to the photographs, the paintings, the knick-knacks which line every table and cluster on every possible surface. One knows that these are the mementoes of a great queen but even the eye of faith is overwhelmed. The association does not raise them. The bric-a-brac forms a typical Victorian interior and one is looking at junk, royal junk maybe but nonetheless junk. It is very heartwarming.

The queen is buried in the royal mausoleum at Frogmore, **Windsor** (plate 25), but it was in her bedroom at **Osborne** that she died, in a bed now marked by a huge memorial tablet of bronze. Her death on 22nd January 1901 was an event which invites a cliche—it marked the end of an era. The old world had only thirteen more years to run and the queen died on the arm of the man who killed it. He was her grandson, Kaiser Wilhelm.

Albert, Prince Consort
Born in 1819; married Victoria in 1840; died in 1861.

Prince Albert's industrious life reads like the board reports of an increasingly successful firm. In 1840 he married Queen Victoria but was a foreigner, born at Rosenau in Germany, therefore distrusted and unpopular. He spent his whole married life educating the queen, earning the title Albert the Good, and inaugurating projects coloured by that particular tinge of aggressive self-improvement and profitability that is labelled Victorian.

The Great Exhibition of 1851 developed from an idea which seems to have been wholly his own, to emphasise Britain's booming prosperity, among displays illustrating the industry of all nations in the civilised world. He chaired its committees as a working member, not as a royal figurehead. The project was originally seen as a foreign plot likely to encourage theft, murder, revolution and the return of the Black Death but its extraordinary success earned enough profit to establish and endow the South Kensington Museum —now split into the **Victoria and Albert Museum** and the **Science Museum.**

After this the prince made himself indispensable to the country, just as he had always been to the queen. In 1861 he visited his son, the future Edward VII, who was lodging as an undergraduate at **Madingley Hall,** near Cambridge. As a result of the visit Albert died of typhoid and the country realised its loss.

In 1867 the **Albert Hall** was erected and in 1876, on the site of the Great Exhibition in **Hyde Park,** the **Albert Memorial,** a brilliant confection of metal and mosaic, gilt, enamel and sculpture, a design based on the Eleanor crosses (see page 15). The prince's statue holds a Great Exhibition catalogue and round his feet is a frieze showing man's progress in art and science through the ages.

The queen was inconsolable and, somewhat eerily, gives the mistaken appearance of burying him twice over. The Albert Memorial Chapel, **Windsor** is at the east end of St. George's Chapel. It contains a white marble effigy of the prince, recumbent and in full armour, but is only the memorial it claims to be. He is actually buried beside Queen Victoria in a sarcophagus of Aberdeen granite in a Byzantine-style tomb house. This is the Frogmore Mausoleum in the grounds of Frogmore House, part of Windsor Home Park (plate 25).

THE TWENTIETH CENTURY

Edward VII (1901-1910)
Born in 1841; eldest son of Queen Victoria; succeeded in 1901; died in 1910.

Interest in Edward VII's life must centre round people rather than places. It is the telling incident that is recalled; never where it happened. Brought up to be perfect, he was human enough not to make the grade. Still, he enjoyed himself, gained immense popularity, had his faults forgiven by the ordinary man in the street, and was even more pleased by thrice winning the Derby.

He was born in **Buckingham Palace** and educated at **Edinburgh University,** Christ Church, **Oxford,** and Trinity College, **Cambridge,** but under a system so artificial as to be a mockery. From 1858 to 1860 he was an **Oxford** undergraduate but lived at Frewin Hall, behind the Oxford Union Society's building, where selected professors gave special lectures to a selected half-dozen undergraduates with a special examination after four terms. The system at **Cambridge** was less onerous and Edward resided at **Madingley Hall,** four miles from his college.

His London home for forty years was **Marlborough House** in the Mall, built by Wren for John Churchill, Duke of Marlborough, in 1709-10, but more recently celebrated as the home of Queen Mary.

If any place is closely associated with Edward VII, it must be **Sandringham,** the estate near King's Lynn in Norfolk bought for him from Lord Palmerston's niece in 1862 with the savings accrued during his minority. The house was built during 1869-70 in the ominous Victorian-Elizabethan style and it remains the royal family's private country home, in no sense a national palace.

Nine kings attended Edward's funeral. He and Queen Alexandra are buried by the high altar in St. George's Chapel, **Windsor.** His Garter banner hangs over the tomb and at the feet of the royal effigies crouches a dog, the king's favourite terrier, Caesar.

George V (1910-1936)

Born in 1865; succeeded his father Edward VII in 1910; died in 1936.

George V was born in **Marlborough House** and, like Henry VIII, succeeded to the throne because of his elder brother's death. He also married his brother's fiancée, Princess May of Teck, who became Queen Mary, for so many people the quintessence of royalty. She was born in 1867 at **Kensington Palace,** in the same room as Queen Victoria. Her wedding dress and the coronation robes she and George V wore in 1911 are in the **Museum of London** collection. Queen Mary became famous for her style of dress and her toque hats: the clothes she wore at the 1935 Silver Jubilee service in **St. Paul's Cathedral** are also in the Museum of London collection.

Their tomb in St. George's Chapel, **Windsor,** bears their recumbent effigies of marble and was erected after the king's death. In true medieval style, the queen's effigy was carved and erected in her lifetime.

Edward VIII (1936)

Born in 1894; eldest son of George V; succeeded in 1936; abdicated in 1936; died in 1972.

The future Edward VIII was born at White Lodge, **Richmond.** At seventeen, on 13th July 1911, he was invested as Prince of Wales at **Caernarvon Castle** where the present Prince of Wales was invested on 1st July 1969. The three carved oak chairs used by the royal family on the earlier occasion stand in the Guard Chamber at **Windsor Castle.**

After a time as an ordinary undergraduate at Magdalen College, **Oxford,** the prince began the usual round of royal duties, using **Fort Belvedere** as a base between 1930 and 1936. The Fort is in that section of Windsor Great Park near Sunningdale but just inside the Surrey border. It was built for the 'Butcher' Duke of Cumberland in the mid-eighteenth century, then enlarged by Wyatville for George IV. It is atrociously ugly but was the prince's favourite country home.

Edward was king for 325 days between January and December 1936, then abdicated. One portrait of him was painted during his reign. It is by Frank O. Salisbury, and hangs in **Belton House,** Lincolnshire, the home of Edward VIII's personal Lord in Waiting during those months, Lord Brownlow.

As Duke of Windsor, Edward lived much of the time in France till his death in 1972. He is buried in the Royal Mausoleum at Frogmore, **Windsor.**

George VI (1936-1952)

Born in 1895; second son of George V; succeeded on the abdication of his elder brother Edward VIII in 1936; died in 1952.

King George VI was born at York Cottage, **Sandringham,** and baptised in St. Mary Magdalene's church there, a building of unique royal associations.

Sandringham was always very dear to him and he died there in 1952. Early in 1969 his memorial chapel and burial vault were dedicated so that now his body lies beneath a black marble ledger stone in a tiny chapel set against a buttress of St. George's Chapel, **Windsor.** It is the latest in a long tradition.

Elizabeth II (1952 —)

Born in 1926; elder daughter of George VI; succeeded her father in 1952.

The future Queen Elizabeth II was born at her maternal grandparents' home, **17 Bruton Street** in London. She spent much of her childhood at **145 Piccadilly,** her parents' London home between 1923 and their accession to the throne in 1936, though the house was recently demolished.

From 1949 to her own accession in 1952 the young princess lived at **Clarence House** facing the Mall. This house links up directly with the state apartments in St. James's Palace and was built by Nash in the 1820s for the Duke of Clarence, later William IV. Other residents have included Queen Victoria's mother and two of her sons, Alfred Duke of Edinburgh and the Duke of Connaught. Princess Anne was born here in 1950. It is now the home of Queen Elizabeth, the Queen Mother.

SOME ROYAL FOREIGNERS

King John the Good of France was captured by the Black Prince at Poitiers in 1356 and brought as a prisoner to **Eltham Palace** in south-east London. This was once the largest medieval palace in England and was visited by Leo V of Armenia in 1385, Manuel II Palaeologus of Byzantium in 1400, and Sigismund, King of the Romans and Emperor-elect of Germany, in 1416. Today only the Great Hall remains, covered by a superb hammerbeam roof.

After years of imprisonment in England, Mary Queen of Scots was executed in 1587 at **Fotheringhay Castle,** Northamptonshire. The chemise she wore on the scaffold is at **Coughton Court,** Warwickshire, and the prayer-book and gold rosary she carried are at **Arundel Castle,** Sussex. Her death mask is at **Lennoxlove House,** East Lothian, with the gilt and silver box which held the Casket Letters. These were probably forgeries but appeared to implicate Mary and her third husband Bothwell in the death or murder of her second husband Darnley. In 1612 her son James I moved her body from the choir of **Peterborough Cathedral** to a tomb in **Westminster Abbey,** deliberately a much more sumptuous affair than Elizabeth I's tomb which it matches across Henry VII's Chapel.

The Red Indian princess Pocahontas was buried in 1617 at St. George's church, **Gravesend,** where the registers record her Christian married name, 'Rebecca Wrolfe, a Virginia Lady born'. Her father's cloak is in the Ashmolean Museum, **Oxford.**

Theodore Palaeologus claimed to be among the last descendants of the last Byzantine emperor. He died in 1636 and is buried at **Landulph** in Cornwall. Still more incongruously, his relations spread as far as Barbados and Wapping.

From 1807 to 1814 Louis XVIII of France, younger brother of the guillotined Louis XVI, found refuge from Napoleon in the seventeenth-century **Hartwell House** near Aylesbury in Buckinghamshire, and his wife died there (plate 23).

Fragmentary remains of the emperor Napoleon's military travelling carriage, in which he rode during the retreat from Moscow and on to the battle of Waterloo, are in **Madame Tussaud's** waxwork exhibition in London. The camp-bed he used on St. Helena is also there. The chair he used on St. Helena is in **Maidstone** museum.

King Louis Philippe of France was exiled after the 1848 Revolution and came to **Claremont,** Princess Charlotte's old home in Surrey. He died there two years later.

Prince Louis Napoleon Bonaparte lived when a young man in exile at 55 Great Pulteney Street, **Bath.** He became the Emperor Napoleon III of France but was deposed in 1870 and spent his last months in exile at Camden Place, **Chislehurst,** Greater London. A memorial to his only son, the Prince Imperial, is on **Chislehurst Common** and another, for long at Woolwich, is now at **Sandhurst.** The boy was a great-nephew of Napoleon Bonaparte but became a cadet at the Royal Military Academy in **Woolwich** and volunteered in 1879 for active service with the British army. Within a few months he was killed in a trifling skirmish with Zulus, and the Royal Artillery Museum in Woolwich has his tunic and surveying instruments. The imperial family is buried in a mausoleum under St. Michael's church, **Farnborough,** Hampshire, and the prince has another memorial in St. George's Chapel, **Windsor.**

Strangest of all these foreign royal associations is Prince Lee Boo. In 1783 the East India Company's frigate *Antelope* was wrecked off Coo-roo-raa in the Pelew Islands near New Guinea. The local king sent his twenty-year-old son Lee Boo to be educated in England but within a year the youth had died of smallpox and was buried in the churchyard of St. Mary's, **Rotherhithe** in London:

> Stop, reader, stop! Let Nature claim a tear—
> A Prince of mine, Lee Boo, lies buried here.

INDEX

Adelaide, Queen 77
Albert, Prince 78, 79-80
Albert Hall 79
Alexandra, Queen 81
Alfred 4, 5
Ampthill 49, pl. 14
Anne, Queen 69-70
Anne of Cleves 50-51
Anne of Denmark 58, 60
Arthur, King 3-4, 17
Arthur, Prince 29-30, 32
Arundel 5, 83
Ascot 70
Athelney 4
Athelstan 5
Balmoral 78
Banqueting House 58, 59, 61, 63, 65, 68

Barnet 23, 24
Bath 5, 84
Battle Abbey 6
Beaumaris 14
Becket, Thomas 8, 10
Belton House 82
Berkeley 16
Berkhamsted 6, pl. 6
Bertha 4
Bexley 18
Birmingham 67
Black Prince 17, 18-19, 83
Blenheim Palace 10, 70, pl. 4
Bletchingley 51
Boadicea 3
Boleyn, Anne 31, 49-50, 53

Bolingbroke 20
Boscobel 62, pl. 20
Bosham 5
Bosworth 27, 28
Bradgate Park 52
Bridport 62, pl. 19
Brighton 63, 74, 75, 76
British Museum 12, 26, 29, 51, 52, 53, 56, 57, 58, 72
Brixham 65, 68, pl. 21
Buckden Palace 49
Buckingham Palace 73, 77, 80
Burgh-by-Sands 15
Bury St. Edmunds 4
Bushy House 77, pl. 24
Caernarvon 14, 15, 81

Cambridge 22, 80
Camelford 4
Canterbury 4, 10-11, 18, 21
Canute 5
Carisbrooke 60, 61
Carlisle 27, 66
Carlton House 74, 76
Castle Ashby 54
Catherine of Aragon 29, 32, 49
Charing Cross 15, 61, pl. 15
Charles I 15, 58, 59-61
Charles II 25, 30, 58, 62-64, 65
Charlotte, Princess 75-76, 77
Charlton House 59
Chatsworth 28, 31, 71
Chelsea 27, 51, 63
Chepstow 4, 29
Chertsey 23
Chester 29, 60, pl. 18
Child's Bank 64
Chislehurst 84
Claremont 76, 84
Clarence House 82
Clifford, Rosamund 10
Colchester 3
Compton Wynyates 31
Conway 14
Corfe Castle 5
Coughton Court 83
Cowdray Park 56
Cromwell, Oliver 27, 60, 62
Crosby Hall 27
Culloden 67
Cunobelin 3
Darnley, Lord 57, 83
Derby 66
Drury Lane 64
Eastwell 26
Edgar 5
Edgehill 60
Edinburgh 58, 66, 80, pl. 17
Edmund 4
Edred 5
Edward I 14-15, 20
Edward II 15-16
Edward III 16-18
Edward IV 23, 24-25, 27, 28
Edward V 25-26
Edward VI 30, 50, 51, 52, 53
Edward VII 79, 80-81
Edward VIII 81-82
Edward the Confessor 5, 13, 15
Edward the Martyr 5
Egbert 4, 5
Eleanor of Castile 15
Elizabeth I 16, 26, 49, 51, 52, 55-57
Elizabeth II 3, 82

Elizabeth of Bohemia 59
Elizabeth of York 28, 29, 30, 32
Eltham Palace 83
Elton Hall 31
Emma 5
Epsom 58
Ethandun 4
Ethelbald 4
Ethelbert 4
Eton 22, 23, 24
Evesham 14, pl. 8
Farnborough 84
Faversham 8-9, 65
Fitzherbert, Maria 75, 76
Fleet Street 59
Flint 20
Fort Belvedere 81
Fort William 67
Fotheringhay 26, 83
Framlingham 54
Frederick Lewis 72
Frogmore 79, 80, 82, pl. 25
Geddington 15
George I 66, 68, 71
George II 71
George III 17, 72-74
George IV 74-76, 81
George V 81
George VI 82
Glastonbury 4, 5, pl 1
Gloucester 4, 6, 13, 16
Godstow 10
Grantham 27
Gravesend 65, 83
Great Malvern 29
Greenwich 30, 31, 52, 53, 55, 57, 58, 60, 68, 72, 77
Grey, Lady Jane 52-53, 54
Guinevere 4
Gwyn, Nell 63, 64
Hampton Court 30, 50, 51, 52, 68, 69, 71, pl. 12
Harby 15
Hardingstone 15, pl. 5
Harlech 14
Harold II 5, 6
Hartwell 83, pl. 23
Hastings 5, 6
Hatfield 54, 55, 56, 60
Hedon 20
Helena 3
Hellen's 18
Henrietta Maria 60
Henry I 8
Henry II 9-11
Henry III 13-14
Henry IV 18, 20-21
Henry V 18, 19, 21-22
Henry VI 22-24
Henry VII 23, 26, 28-29, 30, 32
Henry VIII 6, 8, 11, 26, 30-32, 49-51, 52, 58

Henry, Prince 58
Hereford 8, 64
Hertford 20
Hever 50, pl. 11
Hoghton Tower 58
Holmby Hall 60
Howard, Catherine 31, 51
Hunsdon 53, 54
Ipswich 61
Islip 5
Jacobites 66-67
James I 57-58, 83
James II 64-66
Joan, Fair Maid of Kent 18
Joan of Navarre 21
John, King 11-13, 27
John of Gaunt 20, 24
John the Good 83
Jordan, Mrs. 76
Kendal 51
Kenilworth Castle 14, 16, 56, pl. 16
Kensington Palace 66, 68, 69, 70, 71, 77, 78, 81
Kew Palace 73, 74, pl. 22
Kimbolton Castle 49
King's Cross 3
King's Langley 20
King's Lynn 12
Kingston-on-Thames 4
Landulph 83
Lee Boo 84
Leicester 27
Lennoxlove House 83
Leo V of Armenia 83
Lewes 14
Lincoln 12
London, Museum of 21, 61, 65, 67, 73, 78, 81
Longleat 61
Loseley Park 56, 58
Louis XVIII 83
Louis Philippe 84
Ludlow 23, 25, 29
Lullingstone 32
Madingley Hall 79, 80
Maidstone 83
Malmesbury 5
Manuel II Palaeologus 83
Margaret of Anjou 22
Marlborough, Duchess of 69, 70
Marlborough, Duke of 70
Marlborough House 80, 81
Marlow 71
Mary I 31, 32, 51, 52, 53-55, 57
Mary II 65, 67-69
Mary of Modena 65
Mary, Queen 80, 81
Mary, Queen of Scots 57, 59, 83
Matilda, Empress 8, 9
Matilda of Flanders 6
Matilda of Scotland 8

Middleham 27
Monmouth 21
Monmouth, Duke of 65
Montfort, Simon de 13-14
Moseley Old Hall 62
Napoleon I 83
Napoleon III 84
Naseby 60
National Gallery 19, 74
National Portrait Gallery 28, 52
Newark 13, 60
New Forest 6, 7, pl. 2
Norfolk House 72
Oatlands 51
Offa 4
Osborne House 78, 79
Osric, King 4
Oxford 4, 9, 11, 13, 32, 52, 63, 65, 80, 81, 83
Palaeologus, Theodore 83
Parham House 58
Parr, Catherine 31, 51-52
Pegwell Bay 4
Pembroke Castle 28
Penrith 66
Pepys, Samuel 65
Peterborough 49, 83
Peterhead 66
Petersham Lodge 76
Pevensey 5
Philip II 54, 55
Philippa, Queen 17
Pocahontas 83
Pontefract 20, 27
Portsmouth 77
Prestonpans 66
Public Record Office Museum 6, 12, 18, 28, 31, 53
Ragley Hall 75
Raleigh, Sir Walter 57, 59
Ravenspur 20
Reading Abbey 8, pl. 3
Regents Park Terraces 76
Richard I 11
Richard II 7, 17, 18, 19-20
Richard III 25, 26-28
Richmond 51, 57, 81
Rochester 63
Rotherhithe 84

Rowton Heath 60
Runnymede 12
Rupert, Prince 59
St. Albans 3, 23
St. Giles-in-the-Fields 62
St. James's 72, 78
St. James's Palace 62, 65, 66, 67, 69, 74, pl. 10
St. James's Park 63
St. Martin's - in - the-Fields 64
St. Paul's 77, 81
Salisbury 12
Sandhurst 84
Sandringham 80-81, 82
Scone 62
Sedgemoor 65
Selby 8
Seymour, Jane 50
Seymour of Sudeley, Lord 51
Shaftesbury 5
Sheen 17
Sherborne 4, 68
Sheriffmuir 66
Shoreham 63
Shrewsbury 21, pl. 9
Sigismund, King of Romans 83
Smithfield 19, 54
Southampton 5, 21
South Cadbury 4
Stamford Bridge 5
Stanmore 77
Stephen 8-9, 10
Stirling Castle 58
Stony Stratford 25
Stuart, Charles Edward 66-67
Stuart, Henry 67
Stuart, James Edward 66
Sudeley Castle 51, pl. 13
Sutton Cheney 28
Swingfield 11
Syon House 31, 53
Temple Church 11
Temple Ewell 11
Tewkesbury 23, 24
Tilbury 56
Tintagel 3
Tower of London 6, 19, 20, 24, 25, 28, 31, 50, 51, 53, 54, 55
Towton 24
Trent 63
Tunbridge Wells 63

Tussaud's, Madame 83
Uxbridge 60
Victoria 32, 77-79
Wakefield 23, 27
Wallace Collection 59
Wallingford 9
Waltham Abbey 5, 15
Waltham Cross 15
Wantage 4
Warwick Castle 56, 67, 72
Warwick the Kingmaker 23, 24
Wash, The 12
Wenceslas 19
Westminster 11, 14, 15, 17, 25, 29
Westminster Abbey 5, 6, 13, 14, 15, 17, 20, 21, 22, 25, 29, 51, 52, 55, 57, 58, 59, 63, 69, 70, 71, 72, 83
Westminster Abbey Museum 17, 29, 57, 63, 68, 69, 70
Westminster Hall 7, 61
Weymouth 73
Whippingham 78
Wilhelm, Kaiser 79
William I 5-7
William II 7
William III 65, 67-69
William IV 76-77, 82
Wilton 56
Winchester 4, 5, 7, 13, 29, 31, 54
Windsor Castle 17, 22, 31, 59, 61, 70, 73, 76, 81
Windsor Great Park 73, 74, 81
Windsor, St. George's Chapel 17, 23, 24-25, 31, 32, 50, 61, 74, 76, 77, 80, 81, 82, 84, pl. 7
Wisbech 12
Woburn Abbey 60, 78
Wolfhall 50
Wolsey, Cardinal 30
Woodstock 8, 10, 18
Woolwich 76, 84
Worcester 13, 30, 62
Wren, Sir Christopher 31, 68, 70, 80
Wroughton 4
York 27

Titles in the 'Discovering' series with their series numbers

Discovering Abbeys and Priories (57)
Discovering Antique Maps (98)
Discovering Antique Prints (266)
Discovering Archaeology in Denmark (141)
Discovering Archaeology in England and Wales (46)
Discovering Avebury (280)
Discovering Backpacking (256)
Discovering Battlefields of England (176)
Discovering Bells and Bellringing (29)
Discovering Bird Courtship (236)
Discovering Bird Watching (155)
Discovering Book Collecting (267)
Discovering Canals in Britain (257)
Discovering Castle Combe (5)
Discovering Castles in England and Wales (152)
Discovering Cathedrals (112)
Discovering Christian Names (156)
Discovering Church Architecture (214)
Discovering Churches (137)
Discovering Church Furniture (69)
Discovering Churchyards (268)
Discovering the Cinque Ports (237)
Discovering Corn Dollies (199)
Discovering Cottage Architecture (275)
Discovering Country Walks in North London (240)
Discovering Country Walks in South London (271)
Discovering Dice and Dominoes (255)
Discovering Embroidery of the Nineteenth Century (99)
Discovering England's Trees (86)
Discovering English Architecture (244)
Discovering English Customs and Traditions (66)
Discovering English Dialets (235)
Discovering English Folk Dance (206)
Discovering English Folksong (270)
Discovering English Furniture (223)
Discovering English Vineyards (269)
Discovering Gardens in Britain (56)
Discovering Ghosts (147)
Discovering Hallmarks on English Silver (38)
Discovering Harness and Saddlery (119)
Discovering Heraldry (250)
Discovering Herbs (89)
Discovering Hill Figures (12)
Discovering Horse Brasses (44)
Discovering Horse-drawn Caravans (258)
Discovering Horse-drawn Carriages (194)
Discovering Horse-drawn Commercial Vehicles (224)
Discovering Horse-drawn Farm Machinery (245)
Discovering Kings and Queens (151)
Discovering Local History (158)
Discovering London Curiosities (165)
Discovering London for Children (110)
Discovering London's Guilds and Liveries (180)
Discovering London's Inns and Taverns (243)
Discovering London's Parks and Squares (259)
Discovering London's Statues and Monuments (42)
Discovering London Street Names (225)
Discovering London Villages (215)
Discovering Lost Canals (207)

Discovering Lost Mines (265)
Discovering Lost Railways (178)
Discovering Mahjong (222)
Off-beat Walks in London (63)
Discovering Old Board Games (182)
Discovering Old Buttons (213)
Discovering Old Cameras (260)
Discovering Old Motor Cycles (160)
Discovering Orienteering and Wayfaring (168)
Discovering Place-names (102)
Discovering Preserved Railways (253)
Discovering the Quantocks (195)
Discovering the Ridgeway (211)
Discovering Roman Britain (272)
Discovering Scottish Architecture (278)
Discovering Scottish Battlefields (174)
Discovering Scottish Castles (279)
Discovering Shrines and Holy Places (254)
Discovering Stately Homes (164)
Discovering Statues in Central and Northern England (49)
Discovering Statues in Southern England (31)
Discovering Surnames (35)
Discovering Textile History and Design (261)
Discovering the Thames (47)
Discovering Timber-framed Buildings (242)
Discovering Traditional Farm Buildings (262)
Discovering Treasure Hunting (247)
Discovering Walking (248)
Discovering Walks in the Chilterns (136)
Discovering Walks in the Cotswolds (191)
Discovering Walks in Essex (273)
Discovering Walks in Hertfordshire (170)
Discovering Walks in Lakeland Mountains (277)
Discovering Walks in the New Forest (218)
Discovering Walks in Norfolk (274)
Discovering Walks in Suffolk (263)
Discovering Walks in Surrey (264)
Discovering Walks in Wessex Towns (198)
Discovering Walks in West Sussex (217)
Discovering Wall Paintings (22)
Discovering Watermills (80)
Discovering Wild Plant Names (166)
Discovering Windmills (13)
Discovering Your Family Tree (93)
Discovering Your Old House (14)